Why Millennials Don't Go to Church

Why Millennials Don't Go to Church

Helen C. Trainor

WIPF & STOCK · Eugene, Oregon

WHY MILLENNIALS DON'T GO TO CHURCH

Copyright © 2025 Helen C. Trainor. All rights reserved. Except for brief quotations in critical publications or reviews, no part of this book may be reproduced in any manner without prior written permission from the publisher. Write: Permissions, Wipf and Stock Publishers, 199 W. 8th Ave., Suite 3, Eugene, OR 97401.

Wipf & Stock
An Imprint of Wipf and Stock Publishers
199 W. 8th Ave., Suite 3
Eugene, OR 97401

www.wipfandstock.com

PAPERBACK ISBN: 979-8-3852-4097-5
HARDCOVER ISBN: 979-8-3852-4098-2
EBOOK ISBN: 979-8-3852-4099-9

VERSION NUMBER 09/09/25

Scripture quotations are from New Revised Standard Version Bible, copyright © 1989 National Council of the Churches of Christ in the United States of America. Used by permission. All rights reserved worldwide.

Contents

Introduction | vii

Chapter 1   Millennials' Loss of Faith | 1
Chapter 2   Finding a Reliable Source | 10
Chapter 3   The Influence of Religious Culture | 24
Chapter 4   Jesus' God | 37
Chapter 5   Jesus' Witness | 51
Chapter 6   Beloved of God | 86
Chapter 7   Emergence of Christian Spirituality | 94
Chapter 8   A Risen Lord | 102
Chapter 9   Paul's Witness | 112
Chapter 10   Toward a New Orthodoxy | 133

Afterword | 141
Bibliography | 143

Introduction

I BEGAN THIS SEVEN-YEAR journey in order to explain why millennials want nothing to do with church. It all began after I attended the wedding of my daughter's best friend. The wedding was an intentionally non-denominational affair, even though the bride had been raised in the Episcopal Church and the groom was Catholic. The wedding site faced west toward the Pacific coast, and the bride and groom spoke their vows under the cool shade of a giant California oak. The couple had written their own service and, when it came time for the groom to express his love to his bride, he spoke in Spanish so that his parents could understand at least part of the service. The couple spoke of some of the trials their relationship had already endured and of the challenges they knew lay ahead. The officiant was a friend of the couple, having secured a license to officiate from the State of California for that date.

The wedding feast that followed featured roast pig, fine California wine from local vineyards, and an array of fresh, delicate salads. The bridal couple sat in the middle of a long table surrounded by all one hundred wedding guests. The couple had invited ten of the guests to give short toasts or tributes. The parents spoke first, the bride's father in English and the groom's father in Spanish. The bride's father wished for peace and prosperity. The groom's father wished the couple many sons. Then followed the cherished reminiscences of the couple's closest friends. One Chinese-American man, a co-worker of the groom, spoke of how he loved the groom as a brother. A young woman, who had been the lesbian partner of the bride before she met the groom, remembered the trials of their college years and the adventures they had shared on their first trip out to San Francisco. A co-worker

INTRODUCTION

of the bride spoke of the love between the couple, comparing it to a mutual heart transplant—a reference to the bride's job involving the caring for the bodies of the recently dead until a team of surgeons arrive to harvest the organs. No one, however, used the language of prayer or blessing.

As the party reached its peak, I chatted with one of the bride's girlfriends and her Croatian husband, both graduates of Ivy League schools. The young woman's parents were both university professors, and the family had lived all over the world. She asked me what I do for a living, and I said that I am a civil rights lawyer, an ordained Episcopal deacon, and a vowed monastic. She looked quizzical, so I explained that I am an ordained clergy person in the Episcopal church and that my primary vocation is to lead others into mission. She was clearly at sea. I tried to widen the scope of the discussion by explaining that I am a leader in one of the mainline Protestant denominations. She asked, "What do you mean by a mainline church?" but she could as well have said, "I have no way of understanding what you are telling me." I didn't even try to explain contemporary monasticism.

So, my original thought was that I would write a book to persuade millennials that their values were resonant with Christian teachings and that they should give the church a second look. But, soon after the wedding, I attended services at a local Episcopal church. The sanctuary of the small New England church was stifling hot because the congregation had grown so small that it had to choose between paying a priest and being comfortable during summer months. The front doors were closed to the street. I bravely pried the doors open and picked up a service leaflet. A few hardy souls waited in silence in the pews, and no one noticed me as I took a seat toward the middle. There was a short prelude and then the organist launched into the opening bars of hymn 564: "He Who Would Valiant Be." The congregation rose their feet and droned these words:

> He who would valiant be 'gainst disaster
> Let him in constancy follow the Master . . .
>
> . . . Who so beset him round with dismal stories
> Do but themselves cofound, his strength the more is.
> No foes shall stay his might, though he with giants fight;
> He will make good his right to be a pilgrim . . .
>
> Since, Lord, thou dost defend us with thy Spirit,
> We know we at the end of life shall inherit.

INTRODUCTION

> Then fancies flee away. I'll fear not what men say,
> I'll labor night and day to be a pilgrim.[1]

At first, I enjoyed the hymn as a relic of my childhood. But then I began to listen to its theology. Be strong! Be courageous! In the face of certain disaster, dismal stories, and giants, fight for the right to be a pilgrim! Tally-ho into the trenches! If only we labor night and day to follow our Master, we can be assured that, in the afterlife, Jesus will be there to defend us! Or, in other words, life is awful, but our faith that God will defend us and reward us at the end of our lives is enough to sustain us over our "foes." Could this be "good news," I wondered?

I realized that, as fond as I was of the familiarity with this theology and these practices, I am actually embarrassed by the whole thing. What does the Victorian belief in Christian exceptionalism say to our children in an era of religious interspirituality? Where is the good news in the view that life is joyless and only to be endured in order to obtain the fruits of heaven? Where is heaven, anyway? And what about the language of violence? I had a vivid memory of standing behind the altar at a parish I was serving, wondering what Jesus would say if he happened to pass by and walk into the sanctuary. It would be something like, "What the h** is going on here?" And that was just the hymn!

So, as time wore on, I discovered that I didn't know what I would say about Christianity that would be appealing. I didn't even really understand what the "good news" was. Is it "good news" that Jesus died, rose, and will come again? If so, how and why? Certainly, this would not have been "good news" for Jesus. Or, is the "good news" that I am "saved" by my belief? Maybe, but what does it mean to be "saved"? The questions just kept coming. And I realized that I was in no shape to try to evangelize, much less make sense of what I had been taught to believe. It seemed that the task ahead was not so much to try to persuade a new generation to return to the old ways but to discover for myself who Jesus really is. As it turned out, millennials and I have the same questions.

We are living in a time of intense spiritual hunger, but mainline Christianity is still only offering us a story about someone who lived long ago, had intense spiritual experiences, and died for our sins (whatever that means). Our hunger stems from the reality that *someone else's experiences of God* cannot substitute for personal encounter and that *someone*

---

1. *The Hymnal 1982* (The Church Hymnal Corporation, 1985).

INTRODUCTION

else's teachings about God are meaningful only if we can grasp the human impulses that informed them.

This book, then, follows the path of the journey I took in order to try to understand why millennials are so disenchanted with church. If I could get to the bottom of their doubts, maybe I could get to the bottom of my own. So, I started by trying to define the operative circumstances of millennial lives as they might affect their religiosity. What is it about our age that threatens belief in religion generally? Are there circumstances that are uniquely perilous to the Christian faith? I discovered that, while there are some real cultural hindrances to leading a life of confirmed faith, they might only explain why millennials don't go to *church*. They don't explain millennials' utter disenchantment with *Christianity*.

In the end, it was the question of whether Christianity as it is practiced today bears any resemblance to the two-part revelation of God in the life and resurrection of Jesus Christ that demanded my attention. But what I was really hoping was that I could identify some common basis between Jesus' life and my own that would allow me to believe once again.

I began with the question underlying all biblical scholarship: Is there anything about Jesus that is inarguably true and, if so, what kind of "truth" are we talking about? I soon realized that I needed to try to determine what Jesus' own understanding of himself and his mission might have been within his own tradition—and, for that, I needed to understand how Jesus would have interpreted his startling encounters with the God he knew as "Yahweh" but whom he called "Abba," or "father." This, in turn, required that I learn about first-century Judaism, not only because Jesus would have looked to his own traditions for answers but also because I needed a baseline from which to determine any areas of dissonance between what Jesus would have believed and what Christian doctrine has always taught.

While I am confident I can do justice to this approach, I am not a biblical scholar, least of all of first-century Judaism. But I have been a faithful and, at times, a faith-filled Christian all of my life. I also know something of human frailty and suffering and have had to address those realities on behalf of others and also within myself. More fundamentally, though, I have trusted that any truly honest faith will arise only from our own lived experience and not because someone else has convinced us of some other reality—usually their own! It must have been the same for Jesus—that what he meant arose from his own lived experience. And there is no question that that was overwhelmingly shaped by his own culture and his own spirituality.

Chapter 1   Millennials' Loss of Faith

MILLENNIALS SAY THAT THEY don't go to church because the church has nothing to say to them. They use words like "hypocritical," "irrelevant," "outdated," "authoritarian," and "hierarchical." It would be easy to dismiss these comments—after all, the church has persevered through more than two thousand years of turbulent history—or attribute this malaise to a natural rhythm of reformation that occurs every five hundred years or so.[1] It may well be that reformations of the church occur in five-hundred-year cycles. And it may also be that we are in a liminal period on the verge of a new cycle. But what is happening in our time is not a call for reformation. Millennials today question *the very need for and legitimacy of* the institutional church. And with that comes their rejection of Christian doctrine as entrusted to and interpreted by the church for over two thousand years.

This loss of faith in the church and its message has occurred only very recently. My parents' generation, for example, was indelibly affected by World War II. From that war, they learned about the fragility of life, and about frugality, personal sacrifice, and honest living—and they recognized these same values in Christian scripture and theology. My generation was also shaped by war, as well as by the assassinations of John and Robert Kennedy and Martin Luther King and by the feminist movement. From these events, we learned to be skeptical of the motives of large institutions and of the limitations on our power to make them work for justice. Still, like our parents, we discovered that Christianity spoke to our experience. In it, we saw "liberation theology" mirrored in Jesus' mission, the African-American

---

1. Phyllis Tickle famously calls this the church's "500-year rummage sale." Tickle, *The Great Emergence*.

struggle for freedom and dignity reflected in the exodus, and pervasive chauvinism in both the Old and New Testaments—all of which resonated with our felt need to confront systems of power and to mobilize on behalf of the disenfranchised.

But it is not just that Christianity in its present form is not speaking to our children; they are not even interested in listening. I will explore the role the church has played in bringing us to this point, but, for now, it's important to recognize that the church is not entirely at fault for this state of affairs. It seems to me that there are two powerful social drivers—the Internet and the social sciences—that have succeeded in undermining the church's viability.

The Internet and the Democratization of Religious Truth

Millennials are the first generation in human history to grow up having immediate access to all of the world's accumulated knowledge. It's easy to underestimate what a watershed this is in the evolution of social history, since its technology has now so thoroughly interpenetrated daily, even hourly, living. But the long view of the history of knowledge[2] reminds us that most people, until recently, could neither read nor write and that, until two decades ago, the only resources for the world's knowledge available to the general public were local libraries and encyclopedia salespeople. The Internet makes access to knowledge truly universal, in terms of both the sheer breadth of available written sources and the number of potential users. When it comes to religious and sacred texts, millennials worldwide have at their fingertips a cornucopia of resources about spiritual practices and religious truth. The practices of yoga, meditation, tai chi, and acupuncture, to name a few, considered exotic and even outré just a generation ago, are now common practices in everyday living. Millennials are as conversant with the idea of mindfulness as they are with the downward dog pose. They discover truth as profoundly in the Bhagavad Gita as they might in the seventeenth chapter of the Gospel of John.

This unprecedented capability has two features. It is empowering and it is unmediated. It opens up a wild west where there are no restrictions on the power to learn and no one to guide paths through the wilderness of human thought. It also levels the playing field between lay seekers and professionals. Only thirty years ago, for example, the only way to gain access

2. See Moller, *The Map of Knowledge*.

CHAPTER 1   MILLENNIALS' LOSS OF FAITH

to the law was to find a law library. Even so, mere access to the key source materials—cases and statutes—are of little value in understanding how to apply the law to a particular issue or situation. For this kind of expertise, it would be necessary to hire a lawyer. Now, however, the law is online and so are the tools necessary to understand its applicability to particular problems. The millennial researcher need not rely on a lawyer to answer most questions or to draft many types of legal documents. And, should consultation with a lawyer be necessary, the Internet is always there as a secondary source of information and learning.

The result of universal and unmediated access to knowledge is that it has the potential for upsetting what is believed to be settled or definitive. Millennials now routinely search the web to determine for themselves whether the views of experts, professors, or clergy can be trusted and often discover that nearly every received truth either was or still is the subject of intense debate. Millennials can now easily see for themselves how original materials have been mediated over time so that it is often the expert's opinion about the original sources that is assumed to be definitive rather than the voice of the original authors or editors. A recent example is the discovery of a number of gospels (among other writings) in the 1940s at Nag Hammadi in Egypt and the process that led to their being made accessible to a worldwide audience. When scholars, after four decades, were able to collect enough of the writings for study, they concluded that the gospels were "gnostic" and likely hidden away in the fourth century after gnosticism was declared heretical.[3] The gospels are now known to the world as the "Gnostic Gospels" only because that is the consensus of scholarly opinion. But it is equally possible that an educated millennial, who can now study the original scrolls and compare them with scholarly opinion, would come to a different conclusion—depending upon that individual's understanding of both gnosticism and how orthodox Christianity evolved from the many different strands of Christianity. More obvious is that the discovery of gospels different from the ones assumed to be definitive revealed that there were many different Christianities in flux for three hundred years after Jesus' death and that the decision about which gospels should be considered authentic doctrine and which should not was decided not because

---

3. "Gnosticism" is a general term applied to various strands of early Christianity in which it was believed that there are two gods, an evil god who made creation, and a good god who presides over the heavenly realms.

new discoveries demonstrated as much but because a group of powerful churchmen met and voted until they came to consensus.

It should be clear by now that universal access to knowledge plays a large role in engendering the skepticism with which millennials approach religion. But Christianity is, in many ways, uniquely and inherently vulnerable to skepticism among religious traditions for four reasons. First, Christianity emphasizes right belief over right practices, while the other world religions focus primarily on teaching praxis (i.e., practice as opposed to theory) as the way to transformation and transcendence. There are precisely five lifetime requirements for every follower of Muhammad, for instance, and every Muslim knows exactly how life must be lived in order to achieve heaven. Likewise, in Buddhism, there are four noble truths, the fourth prescribing an eight-fold path. Equally, Jews understand exactly what is required of them in order to remain in covenant with God and with their fellow human beings. Christians, on the other hand, are supposed to live by the law of love—an enterprise that so far has not yielded promising results.

Second, as we explore in the next chapter, there are multiple difficulties associated with identifying what Jesus actually said, as opposed to what the gospel writers *said* he said. In the first place, none of Jesus' teaching was written down during his lifetime, and the gospel texts we now have were written by unknown writers a generation after Jesus died. Moreover, the gospel writers wrote in Greek, a language different than the one in which Jesus taught.[4] The difficulty of determining which sayings are authentic and which are interpolations by later authors becomes clear when the gospel texts are compared, for example, with the Quran, whose textual authenticity is unquestioned (and whose criticism of the Bible is precisely that it has been through so many iterations in translation and redaction that much of its text is corrupt).[5]

Third, everything we know about Jesus is the product of layers of translations. If I read the New Testament in English, for example, I am

---

4. In fact, the gospel writers seem to have gone to some trouble to insert "authentic" Aramaic phrases in their texts. They wanted their gospel accounts to be understood as authentic renditions.

5. This criticism originates in the later developed Muslim *hadith*, a canonized tradition about the words and deeds of Muhammad, rather from the Quran itself. But see sutra 2:79 ("So woe unto those who write the book with their hands, then say, 'This is from God', that they may sell it for a paltry price. So woe unto them for what their hands have written and woe unto them for what they earn").

reading a text that a group of scholars have agreed is the best translation of Greek texts—which are themselves translations of Aramaic, Jesus' native tongue. And then, even assuming it were possible to render exact translations between texts, there is the thorny issue of meaning. Take, as an example, a modern translation of a passage from the Gospel of Matthew that reads, "Be perfect as your Father in heaven is perfect."[6] The passage literally translated reads, "Become whole as our Father in heaven is one." Why is the translated version so different? This is because there is no synonym in English for *teleos*, a Greek concept meaning a current reality that contains the seeds of a future unfolding. Similarly, the English word "sin" is actually *hamartia* in Greek, which actually means "dividedness within oneself." These are not just distinctions without differences. They are vastly different interpretations of what Jesus might have intended to communicate. Moreover, nuances in interpreting biblical texts represent only one among a number of ways of determining their meaning. Indeed, much of twentieth and twenty-first-century biblical scholarship, to be explored later, has been consumed by debates about which extra-textual factors have most affected the process of textual interpretation.

The fourth and final reason why the claims made in Christianity are uniquely susceptible to skepticism is the reality that *no one really knows who Jesus was and how he viewed his own mission.* Apart from the ambiguities that arise from issues of textual authenticity, interpretation, and extra-textual influences, the gospel writers—all of whom were ardent Christians—each had different beliefs about who Jesus was and what he was up to. All agree, however, that even those who knew Jesus best were mystified! For Matthew, Jesus was the new Moses, the prophet of a new covenant between God and his chosen people. For Luke, Jesus was a healer. For Mark, Jesus' urgent business was as a prophet called to prepare Israel for the new age. And for John, Jesus was the embodiment of the eternal Word of God, present with God before time and present eternally in all creation. By contrast, everyone agrees who Muhammad, the Buddha, and Moses were and what they believed their purpose to be.

If those who knew Jesus best were completely wrong about Jesus' identity and mission, it is unsurprising that two thousand years of scholarly speculation has not clarified matters. In point of fact, Jesus' central teachings are objectively mysterious—and not just in the details! It appears that Jesus' self-understanding was that he was a prophet and a teacher whom

---

6. Matt 5:48.

God had tasked with announcing the advent of a new kingdom—one in which God and not oppressors would rule.[7] But there are as many sermons on this core teaching as there are versions of what Jesus meant. And, not to state the obvious, it appears that we are still waiting for the kingdom to come. Jesus' second most important teaching—that faith "in him" brings "salvation" and "eternal life"[8]—is equally mysterious. Does this imply that Jesus meant that all we need to be saved is to believe that he has the final answers? St. Paul certainly thought so. Was salvation even important to Jesus, as a Jew? And what did Jesus mean by "eternal life"—was he promising the possibility that we could live forever?

In sum, the Internet age offers millennials an unprecedented opportunity to discover for themselves which, if any, of the claims of Christianity are true. It opens up the world of biblical scholarship with all of its own unresolved issues, and it reveals the variability of textual interpretations and the ambiguity at the heart of the faith. Most of all, the Internet has placed Christianity in the position of having to compete with every other religion for its legitimacy and relevance in the worldwide marketplace of ideas, just as it had to do when Jesus' disciples first set out to convince an unwilling world.

Social Science and the Recognition of Universal Spirituality

When millennials say that they are "spiritual but not religious," they are making a distinction between religious dogma and the actual experience of transcendence. For them, the doctrines and liturgy of the church no longer offer an experience of the transcendent. Instead, millennials look to daily living to offer up such moments. Their context for exploring and understanding spiritual wisdom and maturation is not the language of theology or of scripture but the language of psychology—of self-exploration and personal growth.

It is now difficult to even remember a time when we as a culture had never heard the terms "denial," "personal truth," or "projection," so embedded is the language of psychology in our daily intercourse. Equally, it is now impossible for millennials to pick up the Bible and read it through the lens of anything other than the psychological insights they have absorbed. Just as the Internet has exposed the fluidity of Christian

---

7. See e.g., Matt 6:33, Luke 17:20–21.
8. John 6:47.

doctrine, depth psychology compels a reinterpretation of every biblical story to mine the deeper psychological truth hidden within them—assuming, of course, that human psychology is the same now as it was in the first century. The story of the prodigal son,[9] for example, was preached in earlier generations as the paradigmatic story of God's mercy to any who stray from God's commands. Today, that story is preached on the basis of the family dynamics underlying it—a younger son in the middle of an identity crisis; a dutiful older son who always did what he was told; and a father whose heart always grieved for the loss of his younger son even as he was grateful for the obedience of the elder—or as a paradigm for spiritual growth in which an all-loving God stirs responses in both sons that lead each on a path toward greater spiritual insight.

So, when millennials say they are "spiritual but not religious," they understand spirituality to be a personal experience of resonance with the inner psyche that can occur in the presence of God, however defined. Within this lie five distinct assumptions about the accessibility of transcendent experience. The first is that God's creation, including human beings, is essentially good—because the good Creator can only create good. For millennials, the idea of "original sin"—the notion that human beings are born sinful—is a logical impossibility. The second is the belief that the sacred is a real dimension and can be experienced by ordinary people. The experience of God is not limited to saints, the clergy, or monks.

The third belief about the sacred that millennials hold is that the sacred is to be, if at all, in the now and not at some future time. Two beliefs flow from this. The first is the belief that the experience of the sacred is not something that can or should be postponed until after death. For them, life is not a series of trials for which the reward is an afterlife in the bosom of Abraham or with the angels of God. Life is, rather, the only platform upon which is being written meaning, value, and joy. The second is the belief that there is no heaven or hell except as ways to describe emotional or psychological experience. Freed of the fear of ultimate judgment and reward or damnation, millennials believe that whatever results from the decisions they make is simply part of a sequence of decisions that contribute to the unfolding of human history and that there are no consequences other than those that play out as part of the human drama. Together, these two beliefs mean that millennials pay close attention to their lives, since whatever of heaven or hell may result from their decisions has repercussions in the now. This is not to

---

9. Luke 15:11–32.

say that millennials are not open to the possibility of some kind of life after death, however. But whatever that afterlife may be, it looks more like liberation from the constraints of living within a finite body than condemnation to a fiery pit as punishment for sins committed during life.

The fourth aspect of the sacred that informs millennial spirituality is the belief that an experience of the sacred is one of affirmation and healing, not self-condemnation and the need for atonement. The focus of that healing is primarily the psyche, which is seen as potentially harmed or even damaged by past trauma.[10] Millennials acknowledge the reality of our persistent and intractable inability to lead the lives to which we aspire, but they see the solution as related to the need for healing rather than condemnation and punishment and firmly reject the church's position that human beings are inescapably ensnared in a vicious cycle of sin requiring regular confession and absolution by the church. Fifth, and finally, is the conviction that the sacred can be experienced through every aspect of our humanity—mind, body, and psyche—and that the experience of the sacred through one aspect of our being heals and integrates the other aspects. Thus, we see the return of body prayer, in yoga, in liturgical dance, and in walking the labyrinth. Moreover, millennials do not believe that there is a hierarchy in the perception of the sacred—that, for example, the experience of unity through perfect alignment in a yoga pose is any less exalted than a moment of pure revelation such as St. Paul had on the road to Damascus. Thus, for millennials, an experience of the sacred is universally available and accessible, always and infinitely possible in the present moment, healing, and holistic.

This explains why millennials, if they go to church, stand mute as the Nicene or Apostle's Creed is recited. It's not just that the creeds speak to the intellect alone and not to the experience of the sacred, or that they are unintelligible even with a theological education, or that they focus on the horrors of Jesus' death rather the abundance of his life, or that they represent a kind of oath of allegiance to an institution with a questionable history; it's that reciting creeds represents a way of "doing church" that is antithetical to spiritual growth as millennials understand it. It presupposes that the churchmen who wrote the creeds had greater spiritual insight than the rest of us. It sets a dividing line between who is "in"—those who profess the creed—and who is "out." And it fails to address the yearnings of the heart.

---

10. See Keating, *Invitation to Love*.

CHAPTER 1   MILLENNIALS' LOSS OF FAITH

Millennials hold up this spirituality against the teachings and witness of the church—about the meaning of salvation, the nature of Jesus, and the existence of heaven and hell, to name a few—and they come up with profound dissonance, even though many of the values underlying their spirituality are core Christian values. Their response has been to throw the proverbial baby out with the bath water—to reject Christianity because the church is no longer a faithful witness either to the values they hold or the spirituality they long for. But might there be a way to disentangle the life and witness of that Jewish rabbi from the dogma of the church and reimagine a church that would actually preach and embody the spirituality millennials long for?

Chapter 2 Finding a Reliable Source

Was Jesus of Nazareth a historical human being, or was he merely the product of the reflections and memories of writers already converted to Christianity? This seemed like the most fundamental question I could ask—because, if there was no "historical" Jesus, I was surely on a fool's errand. It didn't take much digging to discover that there are multiple sources attesting to Jesus as a real live human being. The first-century Jewish historian, Flavius Josephus, mentions Jesus twice in his massive chronicle on the history of the Jewish people. In one passage, Josephus writes of a man "who did surprising deeds" and was condemned to death by Pilate. In another passage, Josephus speaks of an unlawful execution of one "James, the brother of Jesus-who-is-called-Messiah."[1] The Roman senator and historian Tacitus, writing in 116 CE, mentions that the Emperor Nero, who blamed the Christians living in Rome for starting the catastrophic fire associated with him, falsely blamed "the persons commonly called Christians, who are hated for their enormities. Christus, the founder of the name, was put to death as a criminal by Pontius Pilate." These references, and others,[2] were enough to convince me that Jesus had in fact lived and, more compellingly, had made enough of an impression on professional historians as to merit mention in their accounts of his era.

1. See Flavius Josephus, *Antiquities of the Jews*. *Antiquities* is a 20-volume history of the Jewish people, written in 94 CE, the second part of which chronicles the circumstances related to the First Jewish-Roman War (66–73 CE).

2. Other Roman sources, such as Suetonius and Pliny the Younger, also attest to Jesus' existence, his ministry, and his crucifixion. Professor Bart Ehrman confirms that virtually every modern, competent scholar of antiquity, Christian and non-Christian, agrees that Jesus actually existed. See Ehrman, *Forged: Writing in the Name*.

If Jesus was a real person, I thought, that means he has something in common not only with me but with all humans who have ever lived—his human experience. Couldn't the experience of being human, with its attendant joys and sorrows, form a basic assumption from which I could begin to bridge the millennia that separates us? If we really take Christianity's teaching that Jesus was fully human at face value, wouldn't a clearer sense of Jesus' humanity bring me closer to his own self-understanding and thus to what he meant when he taught about the kingdom of God, for example, or reached out to lepers? And, since the hunger for meaning and desire for transcendence is part of human experience, wouldn't Jesus' spirituality also be part of the picture? But of all that Jesus experienced in his day and time, what *specifically* might reveal him as he really was and allow me to grasp Jesus' own unique take on the human experience?

A Jewish Mystic

Unexpectedly, it was during the sabbath prayers on the Friday of a 2018 *On Being* gathering that showed me how I might begin this journey. As the sun dropped behind the towering redwoods, a rabbi intoned the sabbath prayers. Raising the cup of wine, he gave thanks for the fruit of the vine. Holding up the *challah*, he gave thanks for bread from the earth. Then, breaking the *challah*, the rabbi said "Blessed are you, King of the World, who sanctified us with His *mitzvot* and commanded us to take *challah* from dough." No Christian could have witnessed this ritual without thinking of the Last Supper. What if rabbi Jesus, instead of telling the disciples to remember that he had sacrificed himself for them, had said the same prayers of thanksgiving for God's transforming miracle in the *challah*? What if Jesus was reassuring his disciples that, in remembering the example he had set for them, *they*, *too*, could lead transformed lives instead of laying a guilt trip on them about his intended sacrifice?

In that short service of Sabbath remembrance, it hit me that Jesus was a Jew. Believe it or not, this simple fact had eluded me throughout my journey as a Christian. I was obviously aware of it at some level, but Christianity had taught me that Jesus' Jewishness was merely the background scenery that framed Jesus' Christian teachings. So, if I was looking for what in particular might have informed Jesus' teachings—other than the fact of his humanity—it would have to be that Jesus was, first and foremost, an observant, first-century Jew. He was, moreover, a Jewish "mystic"—a person whose experience of God was especially personal, unitive, and loving.

Thus, like any of us, Jesus can best be understood first, as a human being, and second, as a human being shaped by his time and his cultural traditions. Indeed, because Judaism is not just a set of faith propositions but an entire way of living, the significance of everything that Jesus said and did would have been understandable *only within* the context of Judaism. The same holds true for Jesus' spirituality. His experiences of the divine, the miracles attributed to him, even his most radical teachings all have context and meaning within the history and traditions of Judaism. Why on earth had this not occurred to me sooner? The answer to that question would have to await further exploration; for now, I was convinced that I could get a lot closer to Jesus' self-understanding if I honored him within his own historical and cultural context than if I burdened him with the beliefs that arose decades after his death.

So, my task would be to try to see Jesus as a human being within a particular cultural and historical context. I would have to overlook the many gospel depictions of Jesus as a divine being or even as a human being with divine qualities and capacities. At the same time, I would have to recognize that Jesus was no ordinary human being but a person whose sense of destiny and whose connection to the God he called "Abba," an Aramaic term denoting personal affection, was unique and unprecedented.[3]

The Challenges of Accessing Jesus

It turns out that it's not easy to figure out who that mysterious rabbi was and what he believed his mission to be. It is not as simple as picking up the Bible and paging through it to find the right page, or checking its index for "identity" or "mission." The Bible is a compilation of books written over a vast period of time by an array of different authors, and seven-eighths of it is about the experience of a single people, Israel, as they encountered their unique God, Yahweh, through their long history. It's only at the very end of the Bible that we encounter a Jewish rabbi who taught about Judaism in a distinctly different tone and with a radical vision.

Moreover, if Jesus had left us an autobiography, we could just page through it and come to our own conclusions about who he really was. But

---

3. Jesus' native tongue would have been Aramaic, a Semitic language that is closely related to both Hebrew and Arabic.

all we have are "gospels" *about* Jesus that were never intended to be biographical and that were written by people who lived from forty to seventy years after his death! To contextualize a bit, it would be as if my great, great granddaughter were trying to figure out who Martin Luther King was if he had not written a single sermon nor authored a single book and the only resources about him were four sketches of his life and teachings written by people who had not lived contemporaneously with him.

If I was ever going to find my way to a Jesus who could speak to the reality of my own experience, the first challenge was going to have to be peeling back the crust of theology (and cultural values) that obscured him. I was going to have to figure out the difference between what others have said *about* who Jesus was and what he was up to and what Jesus might *actually* have believed, based on his own experience. This turned out to be a multi-year enterprise, because, as noted, everything we know about who Jesus was and what he was up to must be filtered through the belief system and writings of the gospel writers and Saint Paul[4]—none of whom knew Jesus and all of whom were fervent believers that Jesus was not only the long-anticipated Jewish Messiah but also the actual Son of God. In other words, all of the writers wrote accounts of Jesus' life in light of the resurrection and post-resurrection experiences—*experiences that could not have informed Jesus' own teaching.*

But . . . is *anything* Jesus is purported to have taught actually authentic, or is the whole gospel story a work of fiction? This is where the complexities began to mount, as I realized that, even if I used the tools of Jesus' religious and experiential background to determine what he *meant* when he taught, I would still have to be fairly sure that he actually said what he was said to have said! So, as a preliminary matter, I would have to determine what kind of writings I would be dealing with—that is, what genre might characterize the gospels and St. Paul's writings. It was immediately obvious to me, as a lawyer, that, when the gospel writers penned their scrolls, they were not interested in writing either history or biography but rather proof texts of their own Christian convictions. They were looking back at events in the past and trying to create a compelling narrative that would convince a largely pagan audience that Jesus was the Jewish Messiah and that a new kingdom was about to break into history. In short, their writings were

---

4. St. Paul, formerly Paul of Tarsus, lived contemporaneously with Jesus and his followers. He was a respected Jewish Pharisee and initially a persecutor of the new Jesus sect. But he had a compelling vision of the resurrected Jesus and, with that, a conversion experience that uprooted his life.

apologies or briefs, cast in a loosely narrative form. And, since the social sciences did not exist until our own time, the gospel writers would not have asked such questions as, "what was Jesus' self-understanding?" And, "what did Jesus mean by the kingdom of God?" Yet, these were the questions that haunted me. Fortunately, I was not alone; generations of biblical scholars have been asking the same questions.

Thus began a study of various ways in which scholars have tried to identify Jesus' authentic sayings. The Four Gospels contained in the Bible's New Testament are the only gospels—among the many that we now know existed—that were included in the biblical "canon," and so they, along with the letters St. Paul wrote to various house churches in the eastern Roman empire, are the source materials we have.[5] But, here, we come to at least two additional challenges. The first is that of consistency. Each gospel portrays Jesus differently. In Matthew's Gospel, Jesus is the new Moses. In John's Gospel, Jesus is the "Lamb of God." There was even a difference of opinion as to who Jesus was among his disciples—the people who lived with Jesus day in and day out. For example, in the space of just a few verses from Matthew's Gospel, describing the events of Palm Sunday, Jesus is called "Son of David," "king," "prophet from Nazareth," and "son of God":[6]

> Go into the village ahead of you, and immediately you will find a donkey tied and a colt with her. Untie them and bring them to me . . . This took place to fulfill what had been spoken through the prophet, saying, "Tell the daughter of Zion, Look, *your king is coming to you*, humble, and mounted on a donkey, and on a colt, the foal of a donkey" . . . The crowds that went ahead of him and that followed were shouting, "*Hosanna to the Son of David! Blessed is the one who comes in the name of the Lord!*" . . . When he entered Jerusalem, the whole city was in turmoil, asking, "Who is this?" The crowds were saying, "*This is the prophet Jesus from Nazareth* in Galilee" [italics added].

Moreover, all of the versions of Jesus' identity in this text are attested to either by the prophets or the psalms.[7] Indeed, since Jewish kings were often called "sons of God," "Son of David" and "king" might refer to the same individual.

---

5. While St. Paul's letters predate the gospels, Paul never met Jesus nor did he write about Jesus' teachings or witness.

6. Matt 21:1–11.

7. E.g., Zech 9:9 ("your king"). See also Isa 9:6 ("Son of the Most High"), Ps 2:7 ("the Son of David").

Second is the issue of Jesus' own self-understanding. When Jesus was asked who he was, he inevitably turned the question back on the inquirer, or he remained silent, or he told a story that appears to be a non sequitur:

> When he entered the temple, the chief priests and the elders of the people came to him as he was teaching, and said, "By what authority are you doing these things, and who gave you this authority?" [Jesus replies] . . . Listen to . . . a parable. There was a landowner who planted a vineyard . . . then he leased it to tenants and went to another country. But the tenants seized his slaves, and beat one, killed another, and stoned another . . . *Finally he sent his son to them*, saying, "They will respect my son." But when the tenants saw the son, they said to themselves, let us kill him and get his inheritance. So they seized him, threw him out of the vineyard, and killed him [italics added].[8]

Here, Jesus intimates that he is that "son" of the "landowner" by indirection and leaves it to the temple critics to answer their own question.

Moreover, Jesus even contradicted himself about his identity and, on occasion, took actions that were completely contrary to what he taught. In chapter 22, for example, Matthew writes of a conversation between Jesus and the Pharisees in which Jesus appears to disavow the belief that the Messiah will be the son of David.

> He said to them, "How is it then that David by the Spirit calls him Lord, saying, 'The Lord said to my Lord, "Sit at my right hand, until I put your enemies under your feet."' If David thus calls him Lord, how can he be his son?" No one was able to give him an answer . . .[9]

Quoting Psalm 118, Jesus challenges the belief that the Messiah will be the son of David because the psalmist, David, writes that God (Lord) invited the Messiah (whom David also calls "Lord") to sit at God's right hand, and therefore the Messiah could not be the son of David because he necessarily preceded David in time. Still later on, in chapter 26, Matthew recounts that the high priest implored Jesus to reveal his true identity:

> I put you under oath before the living God, tell us if you are the Messiah, the Son of God. Jesus said to him, "You have said so. But

---

8. Matt 21:2–5, 9, 23, 33–39.
9. Matt 22:43–46.

> I tell you 'From now on, you will see the Son of Man seated at the right hand of the Power and coming on the clouds of heaven.'"[10]

Here, Jesus quotes Daniel 7:13 in which Daniel, in a terrifying vision, sees a series of murderous tyrants in the form of beasts, and also

> ... one like a human being coming with the clouds of heaven. And he came to the Ancient One and was presented before him. To him was given dominion and glory and kingship, that all peoples, nations, and languages should serve him.[11]

Thus, as Matthew's Gospel nears its conclusion, Jesus suggests to Caiaphas that he is the Son of Man to whom will be given authority over all the earth. As well, and not secondarily, Jesus famously preached non-violence—yet he was said to have prophesied that he, the son of man, would stage a thundering, cataclysmic return. The gospels say that he was so angry at the temple money changers that he upended the tables where they were doing business. This Jewish mystic said that he came not to abolish the Jewish law but to fulfill it—yet he regularly flouted Judaism's purity laws.

Insights from Biblical Scholarship

There are some 5,000 Greek New Testament manuscripts presently in existence and, thanks to biblical scholarship over the past two hundred or so years, there are now ways of bringing us closer to what Jesus may actually have said and done. This is not to say, sadly, that there is scholarly consensus on the *results* of the application of these methodologies! These methods—text criticism, source criticism, form criticism, and redaction criticism—reveal at least three layers of possible sources in the gospels. The most obvious of these layers was noted earlier—texts included to demonstrate that Jesus was the Son of God. Mark even unabashedly begins his gospel with that statement: "The beginning of the good news of Jesus Christ, the Son of God."[12] The second layer of gospel texts comprises redactions of sources that come from the oral transmissions of traditions and sayings about Jesus. Since the gospels were not written until at least forty or more years after Jesus died, and there are no written sources of his teachings contemporaneous with his life, the gospel writers had to rely on the many oral traditions

---

10. Matt 26:63–64.
11. Dan 7:13–15, 21–22.
12. Mark 1:1.

about him and piece them together in a way that served their narrative. And, finally, hidden deep within the gospel texts is a third strand, Jesus' authentic utterances, most of which are thought to consist of pithy sayings and homey parables.[13] Yet, while this kind of analysis study is essential for the advancement of biblical studies,[14] it only brings us within approximations of authenticity—and it does not attempt to address the murky issue of meaning. That is, even assuming we can roughly identify the texts most likely to have been authentic, how do we understand their meaning?

Overshadowing these approaches is the "historical" approach. Since the 1900s, New Testament scholarship has concerned itself with trying to understand what Jesus might have meant to achieve by treating Jesus' own milieu as the most appropriate (and respectful) point of departure. This approach involves identifying the elements that might have been the dominant influencers on Jesus' teachings and mission. Yet, while there is clear consensus that historical reconstruction is a necessary analytical component, there is disagreement as to *which* historical elements most influenced Jesus' teaching and witness. For Albert Schweitzer, whose ground-breaking book, *The Quest for the Historical Jesus*,[15] launched the historical reconstruction methodology, the most obvious and important influence on Jesus—the one that most shaped his sense of identity and mission—was the heightening of Jewish eschatological expectations prior to and during Jesus' lifetime. Schweitzer interpreted Jesus' apocalyptic sayings[16] as warning of the imminent end of the world and both Jesus and his followers as the universal Messiah for all history.

For E.P. Sanders, writing in the 1980s, Jewish apocalyptic expectation was also the factor most likely to have influenced Jesus' identity and mission, but it was "Jewish restoration eschatology as evidenced by Jesus' baptism by John the Baptist, Jesus' calling of the twelve, his expectation of a new or renewed temple, and the eschatological expectations of the apostles"[17] that were the determinative facts. More recently, Marcus Borg,

13. See Mack, *Lost Gospel*.
14. See generally Collins, *Introduction to the New Testament*.
15. Schweitzer, *Quest*.
16. For example, this passage from Mark's Gospel: [Jesus said] "When you hear of wars and rumors of wars, do not be alarmed; this must take place, but the end is still to come. For nation will rise against nations, and kingdom against kingdom; there will be earthquakes in various places; there will be famines. This is but the beginning of the birth pangs." Mark 13:7–8.
17. Sanders, *Jesus and Judaism*, 326.

while largely agreeing with Sanders, emphasized that the eschatological expectations were not only of renewal and restoration but of the imminent culmination of all of *Jewish history*, bringing about the onset of a new age, or kingdom, and the restoration of the Davidic kingship.[18] For N.T. Wright, arguably our most popular contemporary theologian, *no* single historical element most influenced Jesus.[19] Although Wright embraces the historical methodology, he counsels scholars to consider all possible influences and then ask five questions: How does Jesus fit into Judaism? What were Jesus' aims? Why did Jesus die? How and why did the early church begin? and Why are the gospels what they are?[20] In this regard, Wright argues that New Testament scholarship should be no different than any other inquiry into an historical figure from the ancient past and that his approach has the advantages of taking Jesus' Jewish background seriously, as well as neutralizing political or religious bias.[21]

One group of scholars, called the Jesus Seminar,[22] ascendant during the 1980s and 1990s, attempted to identify the nucleus of Jesus' actual utterances and, from them, make inferences about Jesus as an historical figure. The members of the Seminar used text-critical methods and the Gospel of Thomas[23] to determine which of the sayings attributed to Jesus were more or less likely to be authentic.[24] They concluded, among other things, that Jesus was neither an apocalyptic nor an eschatological prophet but rather a wisdom teacher and miracle worker who died because he was seen as a public nuisance by the Roman authorities. The Seminar scholars also made inferences about Jesus' general *sitz im leben* based upon sociopolitical-economic information that has come to light as a result of archeological findings from the first century. So, for example, these scholars concluded that, since Jesus lived within a day's walk of Sepphoris, a busy

---

18. Borg, *Meeting Jesus Again*, 137.
19. Wright, *Jesus and the Victory*, 87.
20. Wright, *Jesus and the Victory*, 89–113.
21. Wright, *Jesus and the Victory*, 139.
22. These scholars include John Dominic Crossan, Marcus Borg, C. Bruce Chilton, and others.
23. The Gospel of Thomas is one among a trove of gospels found in 1945, known collectively as the "gnostic gospels" because they were written by early Christian "gnostics" or believers who held that salvation comes from receiving secret hidden knowledge rather than through Jesus' death and resurrection.
24. The two most influential of these methods is "multiple attestation" and "embarrassment," i.e., the text is obviously the work of the gospel writer.

CHAPTER 2   FINDING A RELIABLE SOURCE

Greco-Roman provincial capital, it is likely that he spoke Greek fluently, as well as Aramaic. These scholars believe that Jesus and his disciples were peasants and tradesmen. They even surmise that, if Jesus were really an observant first-century Jew (which he clearly was), it is more likely than not that he was married.[25]

Overall, the current state of scholarly investigation into the question of textual authenticity is that all scholars accept the early-source critical methods for understanding how the gospels were constructed and also the text-critical methods for determining what are most likely to be early gospel materials. Most also accept the additions to text-critical methods favored by the Jesus Seminar. Moreover, all scholars believe that historical reconstruction is the methodology most likely to yield credible answers about Jesus' self-understanding and that the appropriate historical context is first-century Judaism. A composite portrait of Jesus that thus emerges from all of this is that Jesus was, and believed himself to be, the one anointed by God (or "messiah") to announce and also usher in a new "kingdom." This new kingdom would occur imminently, preceded by a series of catastrophic events and great suffering, and would result in the fulfillment of God's promises to Israel—that Yahweh would return to dwell in the temple at Jerusalem, and that Yahweh himself would preside over an age of justice and peace. Jesus' mission therefore was to be an agent, or prophet, of Yahweh to prepare Israel to "repent," that is, to be able to recognize the signs of the coming of the kingdom and to be so spiritually reoriented that they would be ready to build and participate in it. In the end, Jesus was put to death because the Jewish religious elite persuaded their Roman overlords that enough people believed that Jesus was their new king that he was a threat to the political order. It is these considerations that current scholarship focuses on in order to determine which of the many sayings and actions attributed to Jesus might be authentic.

So far, so good. Now, I thought, I'm ready to just pick up the Bible and start reading—and all will be revealed! But now loomed the highly politically charged next challenge: Even assuming we can isolate likely authentic teachings from hyperbole, how should these texts be read? Should the gospel stories be read literally—as if the gospel writers wrote God's

---

25. In a recent book entitled *Resurrecting Easter: How the West Lost and the East Kept the Original Easter* by John Crossan and Sarah Sexton Crossan, the authors conclude that the Eastern Church preserved a more faithful, pre-Christian version of the resurrection by showing "universal" resurrection instead of the later Western depictions of Jesus rising from the dead all alone, typically depicted as a vanquishing warrior.

very words through an experience of divine revelation, as the prophet Mohammed is said to have done? If, because I trust biblical scholarship, I could not believe this, could I believe that the oral traditions of ancient times of passing on stories, sayings, and wisdom were so accurate and the gospel writers such canny transcribers that I could trust the authenticity and accuracy of the gospel texts? And then there were other challenges. Did Jesus really mean I should tear out my eyes and chop off a limb in order to remove myself from the tendency to sin, as we are told in Matthew 5:29? Did he believe that all I needed to do to witness the incoming of the kingdom of God was to plant a mustard seed? (See Matthew 13:31–32.) Clearly, Jesus himself spoke metaphorically and not literally!

Moreover, I had seen how literalism could so easily become the *only* way someone might approach biblical texts—to the exclusion of other values. I remembered a time when I was the director of a legal aid project examining possible civil rights abuses in Virginia's prisons and mental hospitals. We had concluded that the private medical provider in one particular prison was violating the civil rights of the female inmates there. But, when I confronted the medical director with our findings, he simply pulled a Bible out of his drawer and thumbing through the pages, came upon a verse from the book of Proverbs: "The wicked bring on themselves the suffering they try to cause good people."[26] As far as the medical director was concerned, the Bible was clear that lack of medical care was just part of the punishment the women deserved. So much for reading the texts literally.

Jesus' Bible

We do not encounter the same challenges when it comes to the Hebrew Bible. This is not to say that Jewish sages have not had plenty to say over the millennia about what scripture means and how it is to be applied in furtherance of holy living! Debating the meaning of scripture is part of a long tradition that Jesus inherited and that continues to this day. But, for my purposes, it came as a welcome relief that I could open the Hebrew Bible—roughly the equivalent of the Christian "Old Testament"—and simply read it. And, whether or not Jesus or his contemporaries would have agreed with me as to the meaning of a particular passage, I could feel confident that they did not doubt its authenticity.

---

26. Prov 21:18.

CHAPTER 2   FINDING A RELIABLE SOURCE

So, the Hebrew Bible seemed to me to be the best way to enter more fully into Jesus' cultural tradition. The Hebrew Bible was the Bible that Jesus knew. He would have been able to read the sacred scrolls either in Hebrew, the sacred language of Jesus' people, or in conversational Greek, the language into which the Hebrew Bible was translated two centuries before Jesus was born. The Hebrew Bible consisted of scrolls grouped into three categories: the "Torah," or first five books of both the Hebrew and the Christian Bible; the "Prophets"; and the "Writings." The Torah, describing God's covenants with Abraham and Moses, contains the sacred law given by God to Moses that formed the basis for Jewish observance as Jesus would have known and practiced it.[27]

The Hebrew Bible contains a hymnal as part of the Writings section. These 150 ancient poems, more familiarly known as the Psalms, were written at various times. Some of the psalms were written as early as 1000 BCE and attributed to King David. These hymns, with the concreteness of all good poetry, express both the joy of believing and the struggle to believe when God appears to be absent, or injustice abounds, or sorrow overtakes the writer. Some of the themes found in the psalms are awe of God and God's creation ("Bless the Lord, O my soul . . . You are clothed with majesty and splendor. You wrap yourself with light as with a cloak and spread out the heavens like a curtain. You lay the beams of your chambers in the waters above; you make the clouds your chariot; you ride on the wings of the wind"[28]); God's eternal love and faithfulness ("Your love, O Lord, reaches to the heavens, and your faithfulness to the clouds"[29]); God's power to bring perfect justice ("Do not fret yourself because of evildoers; do not be jealous of those who do wrong . . . Put your trust in the Lord and do good; dwell in the land and feed on its riches . . . For the power of the wicked shall be broken, but the Lord upholds the righteous"[30]); God's comfort in times of sorrow ("Save me, O God, for the waters have risen up to my neck . . . I have grown weary with my crying; my throat is inflamed

---

27. The Hebrew Bible is not exactly equivalent to the "Old Testament" found in most Christian Bibles. The Christian Bible has 39 Old Testament "books," while the Hebrew Bible is traditionally divided into "sections." Also, the Catholic and Eastern Orthodox Bibles include books not in the Hebrew Bible, called "deuterocanonical" books. Additionally, the order of the books in the Christian Old Testament follows the order of the books in the Septuagint, an ancient Greek translation of the Hebrew scriptures.

28. Ps 104:103.

29. Ps 36:5.

30. Ps 37:1, 3, 18.

. . . The afflicted shall see and be glad; you who seek God, your heart shall live. For the Lord listens to the needy, and his prisoners he does not despise"[31]); fear ("God is our refuge and strength, a very present help in trouble. Therefore we will not fear, though the earth be moved, and though the mountains be toppled into the depths of the sea"[32]); and longing ("As the deer longs for the water-brooks, so longs my soul for you, O God. My soul is athirst for . . . the living God"[33]).

The psalms are unmatched among the world's sacred writings in their candid expression of human emotion—and not just of those emotions we find acceptable. In some psalms, for instance, the psalmist cries out in murderous rage because those with material wealth act as though they are exempted from God's laws.[34] In others, the writer laments about his "adversaries" who appear to have the upper hand.[35] Jesus often relied on the psalms in his teaching and, according to Matthew's Gospel,[36] the very words Jesus uttered in agony on the cross were those of Psalm 22:1 ("My God, my God, why have you forsaken me, and are so far from my cry and my words of distress?"). But, no matter the complaint voiced, the psalmist affirms faith in a God who listens to all of the travails of the human heart and responds with compassion and justice.

Roughly one-third of the Hebrew Bible is essentially a saga of the repeated conquest of Israel and Israelites' attempts to make sense of their God in the midst of that. First enslaved in Egypt, Israel at last came into the "promised land." But, after driving out or making peace with the tribes already residing there, Israel was itself then conquered by the Assyrians, then the Babylonians, then the Persians, then the Egyptians, then the Greeks, and, finally, in Jesus' time, the Romans. Rome would eventually destroy the Jewish temple in Jerusalem (called the "Second Temple" because the first temple had been destroyed by the Babylonians) and, with it, the cultic center of Judaism. Throughout, Israel's prophets railed aloud why God was visiting his chosen people with recurrent disasters even as they also consistently reminded Israel of God's essential goodness and

---

31. Ps 69, 1, 4, 34, 35.
32. Ps 46:1–2.
33. Ps 42:1–2.
34. See Ps 62:10.
35. See Ps 27:2.
36. Matt 27:25.

faithfulness to his promises to deliver Israel from its enemies and bring about a time of prosperity and peace.

Thus, I felt confident that I could rely completely on the Hebrew Bible as forming both the ethical and historical framework that would have most influenced Jesus' teaching. And I could broadly summarize the themes in the entire Hebrew Bible as, first, the yearning of a persecuted people to return to the land promised to them in ancient times; and, second, the conviction that God chose the Jewish people to have a special destiny and responsibility to live holy lives to the end that their God would be made manifest, known, and worshiped by all.

Chapter 3   The Influence of Religious Culture

As I contemplated reading twenty centuries of Jewish and Christian theology, my heart was telling me that it really must be much simpler. I don't mean superficial, just more accessible to the average person. After all, there was something about Christianity that swept through a vast—and completely pagan—empire, and it can't have been the eloquence of St. Paul or twenty centuries of biblical scholarship. Nonetheless, because the gospels do not lead us to any firm conclusions about Jesus and his mission, and because the stories they tell happened so very long ago, within an ancient culture quite different from either contemporary Judaism or modern Christianity, I concluded that, while I could benefit from biblical scholarship, my journey was personal at heart. I would have to trust that my own experience was no different in kind (though perhaps in degree) from the spiritual encounters described in the Hebrew Bible and from those experienced by Jesus. I would rely principally on the undisputed authenticity of the Hebrew Bible, insofar as it reflects an ancient tradition, and learn about Jesus within that context.

Religious Culture

Many years ago, I visited an aunt who happened to live in Jerusalem. My visit coincided with the observance of Yom Kippur, the Day of Atonement. I have an indelible memory of awakening on that particular morning to utter silence, suddenly shattered by the raw sound of a ram's horn, or *shofar*, announcing the beginning of observances. Looking out of my window, I saw that the streets were thronged with people walking with silent footfalls as they found their way to the western wall of the now ruined Second Temple. In that moment, I understood that, for Jesus, Judaism was not "just" a religion. It was a way of living he shared with everyone else he knew and that prescribed a lifestyle that he believed would be pleasing to God.

Aspects of First-Century Judaism

Still, although I've walked the Via Dolorosa and paused to pray at sites believed to be authentic locales of Jesus' birth, crucifixion, and burial, I harbor no illusions regarding the vast and unbridgeable gap between the circumstances shaping my human journey and those that shaped Jesus'. Yet, I believed that, if I remained undaunted by my ignorance of the Jewish scriptural traditions, I could at least identify the most important aspects of the culture that shaped Jesus' belief in God. Most obviously, for example, we know that the Jewish people were the victims of constant invasion, occupation, and deportation. We also know that the Hebrew Bible had been translated from Hebrew into Greek two centuries before Jesus was born and that both versions of the Hebrew Bible were likely in circulation during Jesus' life.[1] Certainly, these facts would have been the baseline for Jesus' teaching and his understanding of his mission.

There are five other aspects of Jesus' religious culture that shaped Jesus' understanding of himself and his mission. The first is that the Jewish people thought of themselves first and foremost as members of specific tribes. And, as is typical of tribal societies, an individual's identity was understood to be based on his or her tribal affiliation and membership within the family. First-century Jews would identify themselves first as a member of the tribe of, say, Judah, and next as the son or daughter of, say, Joseph. So, for example, Jesus would not have referred to himself simply as "Yeshuah" (Joshua) but rather as "Yeshuah ben Yosef," Joshua son of Joseph, of the tribe of Judah (according to Matthew's Gospel). To identify otherwise was to put oneself outside of God's promise of salvation, which was made to Israel as a people, not to individual Jews[2] ("I will be a father to him [Israel] and he will be a son to me"[3]). Without appreciating this aspect of Jesus'

---

1. Known as the "Septuagint," this was the first Hebrew Bible translated into Greek.
2. 2 Sam 7:7–8, Gen 17:7–8.
3. 2 Sam 7:14a, Exod 4:22–23.

culture, Jesus' focus on the value of individual holiness in light of the coming kingdom would seem less startling.

A second important feature is the diversity of belief within Judaism at the time. As a result of its constant upheaval, Judaism was forced to adapt and change over time. By the first century, the upheaval had resulted in a variety of movements within Judaism. The ones we know most about were the Pharisees and scribes, who were basically scriptural fundamentalists while also being open to a tradition of oral interpretation of the laws. Next were the Sadducees, upper-class Jews who controlled the temple rites. Last was a group of radical monastics, the Essenes, millenarians who took issue with how the Sadducees governed temple worship. After Jesus' death, when the Romans managed to destroy the Jerusalem temple for a second and final time, Judaism was forced to evolve from a Jerusalem-centered, sacrificial tradition to the local, synagogue-based rabbinic tradition with which we are familiar today. Thus, much of what Christians call the "New Testament" is actually part and parcel of Judaism's own evolution as it added yet another movement to its core identity as God's chosen.

The Pharisees and scribes were the biblical experts on Jewish law (Torah). They were laymen and teachers and were sticklers when it came to observing Torah—especially the laws relating to tithing, table fellowship, purification procedures, and Sabbath observance. According to Josephus, who was mentioned earlier in chapter 2, Pharisees believed that human beings are responsible for their own actions—hence the importance of strict observance—but that God participates in some way in each action. They also believed that every soul is imperishable and that, at death, the souls of the good pass into another body (resurrection), while the souls of the wicked go to Sheol.[4] The scribes were responsible for writing, preserving, and transmitting sacred traditions. In a society in which most people were illiterate, their expertise was required at all levels of society and government. Sometimes, scribes were also priests[5] and Pharisees. It is unclear why Jesus tended to lump the scribes and Pharisees together, except that both groups were experts in Torah, and Jesus believed that both groups profaned Torah by using it for their own purposes.

---

4. Judaism did not recognize a heaven and hell as we know it. Rather, "heaven" was the dwelling place of God and God's court, and "hell" was Sheol, a place of darkness, silence, and dust—like a family tomb. In Jesus' time, however, the meaning of Sheol had changed so that only the wicked went to Sheol, and Sheol was called "the Pit."
See Murphy, *Early Judaism*, 154.

5. Such as Ezra, who brought Torah from Persia to Judah in the 4th century BCE.

Third, although the Greeks invented the idea of scientific inquiry several hundred years before the first century, nature's course was understood as being directed by the gods—or, in the case of Judaism, by Yahweh God. For example, while Hippocrates is said to be the founder of medicine, ancient Greeks and Romans sought the aid of Asclepius, the god of healing, when it came to curing the sick or maimed. Misfortunes of various kinds were ascribed to an entire world of demon spirits, magic, or witchcraft. These were unintelligible to humans and required special interpreters, such as prophets, seers, or oracles, to discern how the powers of the spirit world might affect people's lives. By contrast, Judaism forbade witchcraft, magic, and sorcery as forms of idolatry (because all power resides in God and God alone).[6] Yet, since bad things clearly did happen, the only way other than to impugn the righteousness and sovereignty of God was to suppose that there was another force at work whose power—though less than God's—nevertheless afflicted humankind. Thus, in the Jewish imagination of the time, illness was not a matter of biological malfunction but rather of moral failing: a form of punishment for sinful conduct inflicted by supernatural forces.

Fourth, and in the same vein, there was no clear separation between the realms of the sacred and the profane. This aspect has two important ramifications for understanding Jesus' milieu. The first is that Judaism makes it clear from the very first chapter of the book of Genesis that everything God creates is either sacred (because God is sacred and breathed his essence into all living things) or reflects God's sanctity (created "in the image of God"). The role of Torah was to ensure that Israel did not violate its inherent sacredness by associating with things or practices that were deemed "unclean." Second, the interpenetration of the sacred into daily life also applied to certain human beings. King David, for example, was called a "son of God" because he was endowed with so many of the qualities associated with God. This is not to be confused, however, with the pagan belief that gods can have relations with mortals and produce quasi-divine offspring, as occurred in the story of Hercules, for example.[7]

Finally, a vital aspect of first-century Judaism is that it enjoyed the respect of the Greco-Roman world because of its ancient pedigree and esteemed wisdom literature. Jews were the only group of conquered people who were exempted from worshiping the pagan gods and—after Augustus

---

6. Lev 19:26.

7. See generally Ehrman, *How Jesus Became God*.

Caesar declared himself to be a god—from worshiping the Roman emperors. In addition, Judaism won the respect of the surrounding pagan cultures because its adherents led family- and learning-centered lives and refrained from the kind of permissive behavior that characterized Greco-Roman culture. Thus, while Israel had consistently been overrun by invading armies, such that its sovereignty was always in jeopardy, its faith tradition, though tested, remained undisturbed. The God that Jews, Christians, and Muslims worship today is the result of Judaism's long and tenacious witness.

The Messiah

There was no consensus among Jesus' contemporaries as to who Jesus was or what he intended. He was variously called "son of man," "the Son of Man," "messiah," "the Messiah," and "king of the Jews," and the list goes on. In order to understand Jesus' concept of the long-prophesied "Messiah," it seemed important to grasp what Israel's expectations about a coming messiah were, both in ancient times and in Jesus' time. Was what Jesus said and did consistent with the ancient expectations?

In the Hebrew Bible, the idea of the coming of a messiah is linked to that of the messianic age. In fact, the Hebrew Bible offers much more clarity about the coming "messianic age" than about the characteristics of any particular messiah. In familiar passages, the prophet Isaiah—writing around 740 BCE, as the Babylonian threat to Israel mounted[8]—made a prophecy:

> In the days to come, the mountain of the Lord's house shall be established as the highest of the mountains . . . [A]ll the nations shall stream to it . . . and say, 'Come, let us go up to the mountain of the Lord, to the house of the God of Jacob, that he may teach us his ways . . .' For out of Zion shall go forth instruction, and the word of the Lord from Jerusalem. He shall judge between the nations . . . they shall beat their swords into plowshares, and their spears into pruning hooks; nation shall not lift up sword against nation . . .[9]

The messianic age will be a time when all wars have ceased and all nations follow the ways of the God of Israel, and when "[t]he wolf shall live with the lamb, the leopard shall lie down with the kid . . . [and] the earth will be

---

8. Scholars believe that there were actually three Isaiahs—one writing before the Babylonian exile, one during, and one after the return to Israel.

9. Isa 2:1–4.

CHAPTER 3   THE INFLUENCE OF RELIGIOUS CULTURE

full of the knowledge of the Lord as the waters cover the sea."[10] The elements of universal peace and universal observance of the laws of Israel's God are the basic elements of the messianic vision, persisting to this day.[11]

The messianic age had additional features, however. A significant number of prophecies have to do with the advent of the "day of the Lord," following which Israel will be restored and returned to its former glory. Before the fall of Jerusalem to the Babylonians, the prophet Zechariah wrote,

> Thus says the Lord, who stretched out the heavens and founded the earth and formed the human spirit within: see, I am about to make Jerusalem a cup of reeling for all the surrounding peoples . . .
>
> And the Lord will give victory to the tents of Judah first, that the glory of the inhabitants of Jerusalem may not be exalted over that of Judah. On that day the Lord will shield the inhabitants of Jerusalem so that the feeblest among them on that day shall be like David, and the house of David shall be like God . . . at their head . . .[12]

The restoration of Israel also involves forgiveness by God of Israel's unfaithfulness and cleansing from sins: "I will take you from the nations, and gather you from all the countries, and bring you into your own land. I will sprinkle clean water upon you, and you shall be clean from all your uncleannesses."[13]

Moreover, at the time of restoration, God's spirit would be given to Israel and cause an inward renewal, spurring exceptional adherence to the law: "I will gather you from the peoples, and assemble you out of the countries where you have been scattered . . . I will give them one heart, and put a new spirit within them; I will remove the heart of stone from their flesh and give them a heart of flesh, so that they may follow my statutes . . ."[14] God's spirit would instill the knowledge of the law so deeply within each heart that there would no longer even be the need to teach it:

---

10. Isa 11:6–9.

11. For example, in his Mishneh Torah, the medieval sage Maimonides wrote, "And at that time, there will be no hunger or war, no jealousy or rivalry. For the good will be plentiful . . . The entire occupation of the world will be only to know God. The people Israel will be of great wisdom . . ." (Maimonides, *Mishneh Torah*, "Laws of Kings" 12:4).

12. Zech 12:1–5, 7–10; see also Joel 3:1–3.

13. Ezek 36:24.

14. Ezek 11:17–20.

> The days are surely coming, says the Lord, when I will make a new covenant with the house of Israel and the house of Judah. It will not be like the covenant that I made with their ancestors . . . a covenant they broke, though I was their husband . . .
>
> But this is the covenant I will make with the house of Israel . . . I will put my law within them, and I will write it on their hearts . . . No longer shall they teach one another, or say to each other, "Know the Lord," for they shall all know me, from the least of them to the greatest, says the Lord; for I will forgive their iniquity, and remember their sin no more.[15]

Indeed, according to the prophet Joel, there will be a day when God would pour out his spirit on *all* nations:

> You shall know that I am in the midst of Israel, and that I, the Lord, am your God and there is no other. And my people shall never again be put to shame. Then afterward [after the day of the Lord] I will pour out my spirit on all flesh; your sons and daughters shall prophesy, your old men shall dream dreams . . .[16]

As well, the day of the Lord will usher in an end to suffering and resurrection of the dead:

> O Lord, in distress they sought you, they poured out a prayer when your chastening was on them . . . Your dead shall live, their corpses shall rise. O dwellers in the dust, awake and sing for joy! . . . [T]he earth will give birth to those long dead."[17]

Out of Israel's dry bones, God will

> open [Israel's] graves, and bring you up from your graves, O my people; and I will bring you back to the land of Israel. And you shall know that I am the Lord, when I open your graves . . . I will put my spirit within you and you shall live, and I will place you on your own soil . . . I, the Lord, have spoken and will act.[18]

Finally, some of the prophecies concerning the day of the Lord also indicate that, whatever good might eventually arrive, it will be preceded by a time of great agony for all humankind.

---

15. Jer 31:31.
16. Joel 2:27–28.
17. Isa 26:16–17, 18–20.
18. Ezek 37:12–14.

CHAPTER 3   THE INFLUENCE OF RELIGIOUS CULTURE

Jesus lived in a time of heightened expectation that the day of the Lord was imminent. As a result, those prophecies became conflated with final judgment expectations, called "apocalypticism." Apocalyptic literature expressed the belief that there would finally be an end time when justice would at last prevail on the earth. These writings were a way for subjugated people to express their righteous anger to God that evil seemed to triumph over good in the world and that righteous people suffered at the hands of oppressors. As just one of the literally hundreds of examples of this kind of outrage, the psalmist writes,

> Fight those who fight me, O Lord; attack those who are attacking me . . . Let those who seek after my life be shamed and humbled. Let their way be dark and slippery . . . They pay me evil in exchange for good; my soul is full of despair . . . O Lord, how long will you look on? . . . Give me justice, O Lord my God, according to your righteousness; do not let them triumph over me."[19]

In the Hebrew Bible, the book that most clearly describes a coming apocalypse is the book of Daniel.[20] The book of Daniel was written in the second century BCE, but its tale consists of prophecies given by its fictitious hero, Daniel, to the king of Babylon back in the sixth century BCE. Daniel was a wise man and Hassidic Jew in the court of Nebuchadnezzar who outdid the king's sages with his prophetic abilities. The general theme of the book is God's sovereignty over history and especially over human conquerors. But the passage that bears most directly on the ethos of Jesus' contemporaries was a vision in which Daniel saw four beasts. Each beast represented one of the four great conquerors of Israel, starting with the Babylonians and ending with the Greek Syrian Seleucids. The fourth beast was the fiercest, representing the Seleucid king, Antiochus Epiphanes IV. Around 168 BCE, Antiochus imposed pagan worship on the Jews and required them to worship him as their god and offer their sacrifices to him rather than to Yahweh. This, of course, would have required the Jews to commit apostasy and so sparked a war (the Maccabean war) against the Seleucid occupation, which Israel won. Daniel saw

---

19. Ps 35:1, 4, 11, 12, 17, 24.

20. Other, non-canonical books were found among the Dead Sea Scrolls in 1948. These books are associated with a radical sect, the Essenes, who opposed the temple hierarchy. Enoch I, written c. 300 BCE, is an apocalyptic story of Enoch, a descendent of Methusalah, and his experiences with fallen angels, divine secrets, and the fate of the human soul.

> ... one like a human being [also translated "son of man"] coming with the clouds of heaven. And he came with the Ancient One and was presented before him. To him was given dominion and glory and kingship ... His dominion is an everlasting dominion ... As I looked, this horn [a horn attached to the fourth beast] made war with the holy ones and was prevailing over them, until the Ancient One came; then judgment was given for the holy ones of the Most High, and the time arrived when the holy ones gained possession of the kingdom.[21]

In this vision, one "like a human being" (possibly an angel or even the archangel Michael) is given an everlasting kingship and dominion over the earth even as the "Ancient One" vanquishes the last and final empire, bringing justice to the "holy ones" (Israel) and an eternal kingdom.[22]

This passage in Daniel is particularly important for a discussion about God's Messiah, for two reasons. First, the recency of the book relative to Jesus' life, as well as the fact that he quoted it when asked by the high priest, Caiaphas, whether he was the Messiah, indicates that the book (or, more accurately, the scroll) of Daniel was well known in Jesus' time. Daniel, along with two other books in the same vein discovered in Egypt in 1945,[23] are both evidence and expression of the fever pitch of apocalypticism during Jesus' life, which was further exacerbated by the final demise of the Jewish kingship by the Romans and the ascent of the puppet ruler, Herod the Great, to the throne in Jerusalem.

"Messiah," or *mashiah* in Hebrew and *christos* in Greek, simply means "anointed"—that is, anyone or anything that is anointed with holy oil for one reason or another. Kings, priests, and prophets were anointed, but so were the temple altar, certain vessels, unleavened bread, and even the Persian king, Cyrus the Great.[24] Kings were anointed in order to receive the *ru'ah* or breath of Yahweh and thus Yahweh's support, strength, and wisdom.[25] The high priest was anointed in order to sanctify him so he could operate in the realm of the sacred.[26] The Messiah, with a capital "M," however, was to be a future Jewish king in the Davidic line who would rule over

---

21. Dan 7:13–15, 21–22.
22. See Levine, "Daniel," 1247–49.
23. See n. 67.
24. Cyrus the Great, the emperor of Persia, liberated the Jewish people from the Babylonian captivity, allowing them to return to Israel.
25. Jewish Virtual Library, "Anointing."
26. See n. 67.

CHAPTER 3   THE INFLUENCE OF RELIGIOUS CULTURE

God's kingdom in the messianic age. He would resemble King David, who united the tribes of Israel into one nation and ruled around 1000 BCE. Thus, what the elders of Israel sought was not a kingship in the modern sense but rather a theocracy. In a theocracy, the king is believed to be God's representative on earth, embodying the same attributes of righteousness and justice. Kings were often called a "son of God."[27] A list of the attributes of the Davidic kings are found in Psalm 72, a coronation anthem:

> Give the king your justice, O God,
> and your righteousness to the King's Son;
>
> That he may rule your people righteously
> and the poor with justice;
>
> That the mountains may bring prosperity to
> the people, and the little hills bring
> righteousness
>
> He shall defend the needy among the
> people; he shall rescue the poor and crush
> the oppressor . . .
>
> In his time shall the righteous flourish;
> there shall be abundance of peace till the
> moon shall be no more.
>
> He shall rule from sea to sea, and from the
> River to the ends of the earth.
>
> His foes shall bow down before him, and
> his enemies lick the dust . . .
>
> All kings shall bow down before him, and
> all nations do him service . . .

Prominent in this list is the responsibility of the Davidic king to act justly, especially as it affects the poor, as well as to be a conqueror of nations and promoter of prosperity and peace.

David was not the first king of Israel but the second. Israel's first king was Saul. The prophet Samuel agreed to anoint Saul in roughly 1050 BCE, against Samuel's better judgment, and then only reluctantly, after the elders of the tribes pleaded with him to appoint a king so that Israel could be as powerful as the surrounding nations. Samuel warned the elders that, if a king were appointed, he would eventually confiscate their land, their

---

27. See Anderson, *Understanding the Old Testament*, 232–3.

crops, and their livestock, conscript their sons and daughters, and impose taxes.[28] Nonetheless, the elders prevailed, Saul was anointed, and Samuel's prophecy came true.

Saul's kingship was a tragic debacle, so Yahweh gave the prophet Samuel careful instructions about how to recognize the king Yahweh had in mind. It was to be one of the sons of Jesse of Bethlehem. David was Jesse's youngest son and a shepherd. He was ". . . ruddy, and had beautiful eyes, and was handsome,"[29] and Samuel recognized in him the attributes of a future king. After anointing David, ". . . the spirit of the Lord came mightily upon David from that day forward."[30] One of the first stories about David was that he killed the feared Philistine warrior, Goliath, as just a boy with a sling and a stone, resulting in the flight of the Philistines.

Of all the kings of Israel, David was Yahweh's favored one and the only king with a special covenant with Yahweh. David always consulted with Yahweh before making important battle decisions and believed that Yahweh always went before him as he engaged Israel's enemies. David also attributed his victories to Yahweh alone: "The Lord has burst forth against my enemies before me, like a bursting flood,"[31] David exclaimed, after yet another defeat of the Philistines. Moreover, the relationship between Yahweh and David was personal and loving. David danced and sang with joy "before the Lord"[32] and ordered the ark of the covenant brought to rest in Jerusalem. After Yahweh promised David that his "house" would last forever and that David's name would be great, David became renowned as the conqueror of Israel's enemies. Equally well known were David's acts of kindness. For example, David sought ways to show kindness to Saul's house, even though Saul and David had a history of bitter conflict and Saul had attempted David's life more than once. "Is there anyone remaining of the house of Saul to whom I may show the kindness of God?"[33] David asked. When it turned out that Saul's grandson, who was crippled in both feet, was still living, David summoned him, promising that he would always eat at David's table.

---

28. 1 Sam 8:11–17.
29. 1 Sam 16:12.
30. 1 Sam 16:13.
31. 2 Sam 5:20.
32. 2 Sam 6:14, 16.
33. 2 Sam 9:3.

So mutually trusting was David's relationship with Yahweh that David could freely express his anger at Yahweh and even commit grave sins without jeopardizing Yahweh's faithfulness—though still incurring Yahweh's wrath. One such sin occurred when David fell in love with Bathsheba and ordered the murder of her husband, so David could take Bathsheba to his bed. David came to recognize how gravely he had sinned against Yahweh, who, in his outrage, threatened to take all that Yahweh had given David away from him. But, after David acknowledged his sin,[34] Yahweh withdrew his threat—but not his just anger. Yahweh saw to it that the child of their union did not live beyond seven days. The rest of David's reign was then marred by more tragedies, including the betrayal and loss of his son Absalom and the fierce judgment of the prophet Nathan.[35] Moreover, following the death of David's son, Solomon, the united kingdom split into two kingdoms, with ten tribes becoming "Israel" in the north and the tribes of Judah and Benjamin becoming "Judah" to the south.

Regardless, David's accomplishments were legendary. He succeeded in molding the tribal confederacy into a nation under one king with power over a small empire. He decisively defeated the Philistines, Israel's primary foe. He moved the Ark and the priesthood from rural Shiloh to Jerusalem, and he made Jerusalem into "Zion, the city of God." He was a larger-than-life personality—at once a charming and charismatic leader and a murderer and opportunist. He suffered great anguish and ecstatic joy.[36] Throughout, he struggled deeply with Yahweh and with trying to reconcile Yahweh's laws with his own talents and ambition. His last words were in praise of God's eternal covenant with David's lineage:

> The oracle of David, son of Jesse, the oracle of the man
> whom God exalted, the anointed one of the God of Jacob,
> the favorite of the Strong One of Israel.
>
> The spirit of the Lord speaks through me,
> his word is on my tongue.
> The God of Israel has spoken,

---

34. Psalm 51 is thought to be David's prayer of contrition: "Have mercy on me, O God, according to your loving-kindness [*hesed*]; in your great compassion blot out my offenses. Wash me through and through from my wickedness and cleanse me from my sins . . . Against you only have I sinned, and done what is evil in your sight" (Ps 51:1–3).

35. 2 Sam 12:18.

36. Anderson, *Understanding the Old Testament*, 229.

> the Rock of Israel has said to me:
> One who rules over people justly,
> ruling in the fear of God,
> is like the light of morning,
> like the sun rising on a cloudless morning,
> gleaming from the rain on the grassy land . . . [37]

David's lineage did indeed last through multiple kingships for the next four hundred years, but it ended for good when Jerusalem was captured in 586 BCE by the Babylonian empire, and the residents of Judah were transported to Babylon. As with many larger-than-life personalities, David's legacy—his exploits, his piety, and his accomplishments—became the legend of stories, songs, and myth. Even though the Davidic house did die out, Yahweh's promise of an eternal covenant with David's house lived on in Israel's memory and became the basis for hope despite thousands of years of subjugation. Someday, the prophets sang, someday, Yahweh will finally honor his promise and will appoint a king as gifted and as mighty as David. Israel would at last be free to live out Yahweh's promises to Moses.

---

37. 2 Sam 23:1–4.

Chapter 4   Jesus' God

WE FIRST MEET YAHWEH in the book of Genesis as the Creator of everything that exists. This God is a living Presence, giving his "breath of life"[1] to every living thing. He has made humankind "in his image." He has blessed everything he has created as "good" and "very good."[2] This wonder and awe of God's creation and of God as creator is built into the very life of the Jewish community through the sacred laws protecting the fruitfulness of the land, the praises of private prayer and temple celebrations, and the weekly and seasonal rites of thanksgiving for God's blessing and bounty. One of the most beautiful expressions of this wonder is found in Psalm 8: "When I consider your heavens, the work of your fingers, the moon and the stars you have set in their courses, what is man that you should be mindful of him?"[3] Here, to "consider" something is not merely to glance at it but to really gaze at it, ponder it, come to know it, and ultimately see in it the reflection of its Maker.

I remember telling my seminary Old Testament professor that I didn't feel as though I needed to even read the New Testament to learn more about the character of Jesus' God, so awesome was God's portrayal in the Old. This God, whose "name" was given to the great prophet, Moses, as YAHWEH, is without form and deeply mysterious. The very name "Yahweh" is simply a reconstruction from four consonants in the Hebrew alphabet, meaning "I am that I am." Yahweh creates all that is (so that everything belongs to Yahweh and not to us) but also graciously gives all

1. Gen 1:30.
2. Gen 1:31.
3. Ps 8:4–5.

that he[4] has created to the entrustment of human beings. Yet, Yahweh remains sovereign over all so that nature responds to his command, either to destroy ("The Lord, God of hosts, he who touches the earth and it melts, and all who live in it mourn, and all of it rises like the Nile and sinks again, like the Nile of Egypt . . ."[5]) or to restore:

> I will restore the fortunes of my people Israel, and they shall rebuild the ruined cities and inhabit them; they shall plant vineyards and drink their wine, and they shall make gardens and eat their fruit. I will plant them upon their land, and they shall never again be plucked up out of the land that I have given them, says the Lord your God.[6]

God's sovereignty over all has important implications for understanding the entire sacrificial system that Jesus knew and respected and, even more strikingly, explains how profoundly monotheist Judaism was and is. Yahweh, as sovereign and creator of all, cannot by definition share his divinity with anyone or anything: "I am the Lord, that is my name; my glory I give to no other . . ."[7] Moreover, the Jewish people, like all tribal peoples of antiquity, did not start with monotheism in the beginning. Their earliest sense of God was the "God of the Fathers," by whom they meant the God of their ancient ancestors, Abraham, Isaac, and Jacob. Until God's revelation of God's nature as "YAHWEH" to Moses,[8] this "God of the Fathers," though the most holy and powerful, was just one among other gods that were worshiped.

Yahweh's Holiness

Other than Yahweh's holy name, too sacred to be uttered, there are three additional important aspects of his holiness. The first of these is the gift of the law, Yahweh's greatest gift to Israel. The "law," beginning with the Ten Commandments, and followed by 613 laws governing all aspects of daily

---

4. I have taken the liberty of referring to Yahweh as a "he," using the male pronoun. Jesus would not have even uttered the holy name and, if I were an observant Jew, I would refer to Yahweh as G–d.

5. Amos 9:5–7.

6. Amos 9:14–15.

7. Isa 42:8.

8. In ancient times, a "name" was not simply a moniker but expressed the very essence or nature of the person named.

life,[9] were designed to safeguard Israel's holiness by requiring Israel, first, to honor Yahweh's holiness and, second, to treat Yahweh's creation—the natural world and humankind—with care and gratitude. The first four of the Ten Commandments ensure that the chosen people remember and worship Yahweh as holy, "You shall have no other gods before me," and forbid the worship of anything else: "You shall not make for yourself an idol . . . or bow down to them or worship them."[10] Nor may Yahweh's chosen misuse the holy name, use it in blasphemy, or use it to do evil. "Thus you shall keep my commandments and observe them: I am the Lord. You shall not profane my holy name, that I may be sanctified among the people of Israel: I am the Lord; I sanctify you, I who brought you out of the land of Egypt to be your God: I am the Lord."[11]

To revere Yahweh as holy is also to treat others as you would have them treat you.[12] Thus, the last six of the Ten Commandments and the laws given to Moses at a later time require Israel to show love and respect to others, as well to the land and to livestock. For example, the people of Israel may not cheat each other or lie;[13] they may not reap all of the produce of their fields, so that the poor may glean the rest;[14] they may not have sexual relations with kin; and they must not oppress the aliens that reside in the land, but rather love them.[15] Moreover, crops are to be rotated so that the fertility of the land may be preserved, and animals are to be slaughtered humanely.[16]

Just as Yahweh is holy, so has Yahweh issued specific instructions to ensure that the chosen people remain "clean," or "pure." Contact with anything unclean—such as certain types of animals and fish, women during their menstrual periods or after birth, men after emissions, the blood of any animal, people with various skin diseases—required ritual cleansing. For example, Yahweh ordains that ". . . the life of every creature—its blood is its life; therefore I have said to the people of Israel: You shall not eat the blood of any creature . . . ; whoever eats it shall . . . wash their clothes, and bathe

---

9. Most of these laws are found in the book of Leviticus.
10. Exod 20:4.
11. Lev 22:31–33.
12. Lev 19:18.
13. Lev 25:14.
14. Lev 23:22.
15. Lev 19:30.
16. Deut 12:21.

themselves in water, and be unclean until the evening; then they shall be clean. But if they do not wash themselves or bathe their body, they shall bear their guilt."[17] This is not to say that humankind is somehow inherently sinful; rather, all aspects of Yahweh's creation serve an essential purpose, each within its own class. The essential purpose served by Israel is to try to approach the purity and wholeness of God. To be a pious Jew means being marked through the rite of circumcision with a sign of belonging to a people chosen by God to be holy as God is holy. And priests, who alone could enter the most sacred dwelling place of God, were required to have no physical blemish or infirmity, lest they defile the perfect sanctity of God.[18]

A second aspect of God's holiness is God's gift of the Sabbath. The Sabbath is like a bride and its celebration like a wedding. Indeed, the Hebrew word for betrothal or marriage is *sanctification*. Thus, at the beginning of the service on the eve of the Sabbath, Jews recall, "Thou has sanctified the seventh day" and at the end, they affirm, "Thou art one" to parallel the consummation of the marriage by which the bride and groom are united.[19] According to Rabbi Abraham Heschel, the Sabbath sanctifies time itself:

> While Jewish tradition offers us no definition of the concept of eternity, it tells us how to experience the taste of eternity or eternal life within time. Eternal life does not grow away from us; it is "planted within us," growing beyond us. The world to come is not only a posthumous condition, dawning upon the soul on the morrow after its departure from the body. The essence of the world to come is Sabbath eternal, and the seventh day has the flavor of the seventh heaven and was given as a foretaste of the world to come; *ot hi le-'olam*, a token of eternity.[20]

A transcendently holy and passionate God required a suitable place where God could be worshiped. In the days of the ancestors, God was worshiped at various shrines set up to commemorate His gracious deeds.[21] While the Israelites were on their way to the land of Canaan (the "promised land"), Yahweh was believed to be present in a portable shrine, called an "ark." The

17. Lev 17:13–16.

18. There is much debate among scholars as to the reason for the purity laws, ranging from the belief that there were designed for hygiene and public health to the conviction that a tainted food has a damaging effect on the soul. See generally Silber, *Jewish Dietary Laws*.

19. Heschel, *Sabbath*, 55.

20. Heschel, *Sabbath*, 74.

21. Shechem and Beersheba are perhaps the best known.

ark was a golden chest, containing some of the tablets of the law, protected by a gold cover that served as Yahweh's "mercy seat." On either side of the mercy seat were the figures of two angels, their wings outspread over the mercy seat. When Israel was journeying, the ark was carried in front of the people, serving as their vanguard. When Israel was not on the move, the ark was housed in a tent or "tabernacle." Yahweh was thus always present with the chosen people, serving as the focus of their worship at rest, as their guide in their long journey to Canaan, and finally as the "holy of holies" permanently housed within a glorious temple in Jerusalem. Thus, the temple and its cultic practices are a third aspect of God's holiness.

Yahweh's Promises

Judaism has no body of theological truths to which all Jews subscribe. It does, however, contain a central promise:

> But now thus says the Lord, he who created you, O Jacob, he who formed you, O Israel. Do not fear, for I have redeemed you; I have called you by name, you are mine. When you pass through the waters, I will be with you; and through the rivers, they shall not overwhelm you; when you walk through fire you shall not be burned . . . For I am the Lord your God, the Holy One of Israel, your Savior . . .[22]

Judaism is thus a unique *relationship* with God and a *way of life* ordained by God so that Israel might be "light to the nations"[23] and a "holy priesthood."[24] This aspect of God's holiness has three features that would have informed Jesus' teaching. The first is that God's promises are covenantal in nature. Thus, God lovingly extends Himself to his chosen people so that they may "know" him and conform their actions to His will. Scholars have identified two forms of covenant made by God: the "vassal or suzerainty" treaty and the "royal grant." Both types contain assurances of blessings and curses, and both presuppose inequality between the parties to the covenant. The "royal

---

22. Isa 43:1–5.

23. Isa 42:6.

24. Judaism does, however, have an ancient and venerated tradition of questioning and debating Yahweh's laws. This practice has produced the *mishna*, interpretations of the laws as they might apply to new or different situations. In this way, Judaism has been able to evolve and adapt itself to the many different circumstances in which the Jewish people have found themselves over the millennia.

grant" covenant is unconditional and extended to those few individuals who, though not necessarily perfectly righteous, are chosen because they love God and are deemed by God to be gifted to carry out God's purposes.

Thus, God's covenants with Abraham and David were royal grant covenants. As a reward for Abraham's faithfulness, God promises the gifts of descendants, land, and blessing.

> Now the Lord said to Abram, ". . . I am God Almighty; walk before me, and be blameless. And I will make my covenant between me and you, and will make you exceedingly numerous . . . As for me, this is my covenant with you: You shall be the ancestor of a multitude of nations. No longer shall your name be Abram, but your name shall be Abraham, for I have made you the ancestor of a multitude of nations . . . And I will give to you, and to your offspring after you, all the land of Canaan, for a perpetual holding; and I will be their God."[25]

To David, Yahweh renewed his promises to Abraham and promised that, although David would not be the one chosen to erect a temple in Jerusalem, Yahweh would establish a dynasty for David, and David's offspring would rule in peace and in perpetuity:

> Thus says the Lord of hosts: I took you from the pasture, from following the sheep to be prince over my people Israel; and I have been with you wherever you went, and have cut off all your enemies from before you; and I will make for you a great name, like the name of the great ones of the earth. And I will appoint a place for my people Israel and will plant them, so that they may live in their own place, and be disturbed no more . . .
>
> Moreover the Lord declares to you that the Lord will make you a house. When your days are fulfilled and you lie down with your ancestors, I will raise up your offspring after you, who shall come forth from your body, and I will establish his kingdom. He shall build a house for my name, and I will establish the throne of his kingdom forever. I will be a father to him, and he shall be a son to me . . .[26]

By contrast, the covenant between Yahweh and Moses was the suzerainty type and thus conditional. In order for God's gracious promises to

---

25. Gen 17:3–6, 8–9.
26. 2 Sam 7:8–14.

CHAPTER 4 JESUS' GOD

Israel to be fulfilled, Israel must lead a holy life and be a blessing to all nations, as specified in the laws given to Moses:[27]

> You have seen what I did to the Egyptians, and how I bore you on eagles' wings and brought you to myself. Now therefore, if you obey my voice and keep my covenant, you shall be my treasured possession out of all the peoples. Indeed, the whole earth is mine, but you shall be for me a priestly kingdom and a holy nation. These are the words that you shall speak to the Israelites.[28]

Within these promises, Israel is to be Yahweh's "first-born son"[29] and the "first fruits of the harvest."[30] With Israel, Yahweh desires a reciprocal relationship in which God shows love and mercy and Israel responds with thanksgiving, honor, and obedience. The term that characterizes this reciprocal relationship is *hesed*, or loving-kindness.[31] Yahweh freely offers His loving-kindness because *hesed* is part of God's very nature. A relationship of *hesed* is as intimate as the relationship between parent and child. Moses admonishes the people: "The Lord your God goes before you, is the one who will fight for you . . . and in the wilderness, where you saw how the Lord your God carried you, just as one carries a child . . ."[32] In Psalm 103:13, the psalmist also writes, "As a father cares for his children, so does the Lord care for those who fear him." It is like a bridegroom and bride: "For your Maker is your husband, the Lord of hosts is his name . . ."[33] announces the prophet Isaiah. "Can a girl forget her ornaments, or a bride her attire? Yet my people have forgotten me, days without number," warns the

---

27. Yahweh does not add promises beyond those made to Abraham. See Deut 1:8, 11; 4:37–38; Josh 1:2–6, Ps 105:8–11, Jer 3:18.

28. Exod 19:4–6. See also Deut 7:6, 14:2, 26:18 (emphasizing Israel as Yahweh's special treasure and the giving of the law as the means by which Israel will become Yahweh's holy people).

29. Exod 4:22; Jer 31:9.

30. Jer 2:3.

31. That Israel is God's chosen people does not imply that other nations are not also part of God's family and harvest. Rather, Moses instructs the Israelites that "heaven and the heaven of heavens belong to the Lord your God, the earth with all that is in it, yet the Lord has set his heart in love on your ancestors . . ." (Deut 10:14). The Psalms proclaim, again and again, that God is Lord of all of "the nations" and his glory is manifest both on earth and in the heavens.

32. Deut 1:31.

33. Isa 54:5.

prophet Jeremiah.[34] These are powerful images of both deep love and deep desire for the beloved. Thus, betrayal of this love causes Yahweh equally deep anguish and sorrow:

> What wrong did your ancestors find in me that they went far from me, and went after worthless things, and became worthless themselves? They did not say, "Where is the Lord who brought us up from the land of Egypt, who led us in the wilderness, in a land of deserts and pits, in a land of drought and deep darkness . . . I brought you into a plentiful land to eat its fruits and its good things. But when you entered you defiled my land, and made my heritage an abomination . . .
> Be appalled, O heavens, at this, be shocked, be utterly desolate, says the Lord, for my people have committed two evils: they have forsaken me, the fountain of living water, and dug out cisterns for themselves, cracked cisterns that can hold no water . . .[35]

The most poignant of Yahweh's laments is occasioned when Israel forsakes Yahweh for other gods, including Baal, the bull god of fertility worshiped by the Canaanites:

> On that day, says the Lord, you will call me, "My husband" and no longer will you call me, "My Baal." For I will remove the names of the Baals from her [Israel's] mouth . . . I will make for you a covenant on that day with the wild animals, the birds of the air, and the creeping things of the ground; and I will abolish the bow, the sword, and war from the land; and I will make you lie down in safety. And I will take you for my wife forever; I will take you for my wife in righteousness and in justice, in steadfast love, and in mercy . . .[36]

If Israel responds with faithfulness equal to Yahweh's, the covenant is eternal. But, even if Israel completely forsakes Yahweh, Yahweh, though betrayed and anguished, remains faithful, showing mercy and compassion. "I had thought you would call me, My Father, and would not turn from following me. Instead, as a faithless wife leaves her husband, so you have been faithless to me, O House of Israel . . . Return, O faithless children, I will heal your faithlessness."[37]

---

34. Jer 2:32.
35. Jer 1:4–13; 3:12–13.
36. Hos 2:16–20.
37. Jer 3:19, 22.

Last of the aspects of Yahweh's promises that bear mention is their universal application. While Yahweh bound himself to Israel in certain ways, he is also in relationship with *all* humankind. From the first rustlings of His presence as He walks in his gorgeous garden, to His regret of having created humankind and then reconsidering, to His choice of Abraham to be the father of all nations, Yahweh is always and inextricably involved in everything and everyone he has created. "Be joyful in God, all you lands; sing the glory of his Name; sing the glory of his praise . . . All the earth bows down before you, sings to you, sings out your Name," writes the psalmist.[38] And again, "Let the nations be glad and sing for you, for you judge the peoples with equity and guide all the nations upon earth."[39]

Yahweh also offers himself as a covenantal partner to all humankind. God's first covenantal relationship was extended to Noah, on behalf of all humankind; then to Abraham, also on behalf of all humankind, but with special promises for Abraham's offspring; then to Israel, as the people "elected" to lead all humankind into the fullness of relationship with Yahweh; and finally to David, through whom Yahweh would anoint an individual to bring all of Yahweh's promises to Israel to fulfillment and usher in an age of prosperity, holiness, peace, and justice for all humankind.[40]

Yahweh's Justice

As much as the nature of Yahweh is loving kindness, it is also one of justice. In the Hebrew Bible, Yahweh's justice is called "righteousness." The most fundamental response of Israel to Yahweh's righteousness is to love Yahweh: "Hear, O Israel: The Lord is our God, the Lord alone. You shall love the Lord your God with all your heart, and with all your soul, and with all your might."[41] Equally, loving God means treating God's creation with love: "You shall not take vengeance or bear a grudge against any of your people, but you shall love your neighbor as yourself: I am the

---

38. Ps 66:1, 3.

39. Ps 67:4.

40. There are six or seven covenants in the Bible, depending on which source you read: Edenic, Adamic, Noahic, Abrahamic, Mosaic, Davidic, and the new covenant of Jesus Christ.

41. Deut 6:4–5.

Lord."[42] True love of God necessarily entails true love of one's neighbor—the two are inseparable.

There are two aspects to Yahweh's justice: His Lordship and his judgment. The prophets often use the term "fear" to denote Israel's primary covenantal duty toward God, with the result that Yahweh is misunderstood as "fearful," even cruel. But "fear" in this context does not mean "to be afraid of." Rather, it is a term that connotes the only possible response to the utter sovereignty, righteousness, and Lordship of God: a combination of awe, adoration, reverence, and confidence. Indeed, Israel's prophets played the unique role of calling Israel to account for her actions and warning her of the consequences that would follow if she did not "fear" God. "Does disaster befall a city, unless the Lord has done it? Surely the Lord God does nothing without revealing his secret to his servants the prophets. The lion has roared; who will not fear? The Lord God has spoken; who can but prophesy?" writes the prophet Amos.[43]

The most powerful aspect of God's Lordship is that Yahweh is Lord of history. When Israel abandons Yahweh by violating His laws, Yahweh manipulates natural and political events in order to chastise Israel. The prophets could not be more explicit on this point. For example, Jeremiah, writing just prior to the sack of Judah by the Babylonians in 587 BCE, warns,

> At that time it will be said to this people and to Jerusalem: A hot wind comes from me out of the bare heights in the desert toward my poor people . . . O Jerusalem, wash your heart clean of wickedness so that you may be saved. How long shall your evil schemes lodge within you? For a voice declares from Dan and proclaims disaster from Mount Ephraim. Tell the nations, "Here they are!" Proclaim against Jerusalem, "Besiegers come from a distant land; they shout against the cities of Judah. They have closed in around her like watchers of a field, because she has rebelled against me," says the Lord. Your ways and your doings have brought this upon you . . . [44]

The view of history as an instrument of God's justice is entirely consistent with the nature of the conditional covenant between Yahweh and Israel: A breach of the covenant by one party justifies abrogation of the covenant by

---

42. Lev 19:18.
43. Amos 3:6–9.
44. Jer 4:11–18.

the other party. And, when the "other party" is the Lord of history, abrogation can mean captivity, destruction, or worse.

Justice requires judgment, of course, and judgment implies the existence of sin and the need for righteous punishment. In Judaism, Yahweh's will for humankind is perfectly captured in the Torah, and perfect obedience to the law will bring Israel the promises noted above. Unfortunately, as the Hebrew Bible makes painfully clear, humans inevitably fall short of perfect obedience—intentionally in some cases but unintentionally in most others. "Against you only have I sinned," the psalmist confesses.[45] At the same time, righteous punishment always contains the element of mercy. Yahweh is ready to spare Israel at the least sign of her forgoing her idolatrous or sinful ways: "Return, faithless Israel, says the Lord. I will not look on you in anger for I am merciful, says the Lord. I will not be angry forever. Only acknowledge your guilt, that you have rebelled against the Lord your God . . . ," pleads the prophet Jeremiah.[46] Indeed, mercy is part and parcel of *hesed*, Yahweh's steadfast love:

> The Lord is merciful and gracious, slow to anger and abounding in steadfast love. He will not always accuse, nor will he keep his anger forever. He does not deal with us according to our sins . . . For as the heavens are high above the earth, so great is his steadfast love towards those who fear him; as far as the east is from the west, so far he removes our transgressions from us . . . As a father has compassion for his children, so the Lord has compassion for those who fear him. For he knows how we were made; he remembers that we are dust.[47]

Of particular concern to God is the plight of the poor, the widowed, and the orphan—that is, those with no means of support other than through the generosity of others. There are literally hundreds of references in the Hebrew Bible of Yahweh's concern for the poor: "The poor and the needy search for water, but there is none; their tongues are parched with thirst. But I, the Lord, will answer them . . . I will not forsake them."[48] Yahweh is, above all, concerned that the poor have enough to sustain themselves: "Do not go over your vineyard a second time or pick up grapes that have

---

45. Ps 51:4.
46. Jer 3:11–14.
47. Ps 103:8–14.
48. Isa 41:17.

fallen. Leave them for the poor and the alien . . ."[49] and again, ". . . If one of your countrymen becomes poor and is unable to support himself among you, help him as you would an alien or a temporary resident, so he can continue to live among you . . ."[50] Moreover, a righteous God requires that the poor be treated justly: "Because of the oppression of the weak and the groaning of the needy, I will now arise, says the Lord. I will protect them from those who malign them . . ."[51] and again, "Hear this, you cows of Bashan on Mount Samaria, you women who oppress the poor and crush the needy and say to your husbands, 'Bring us some drinks!' The Lord God has sworn by his holiness: The time is surely coming upon you when they shall take you away with hooks . . ."[52]

The Hebrew Bible views just punishment as the familiar phrase ". . . [A]n eye for an eye, a tooth for a tooth, a hand for a hand, a foot for a foot, a burn for a burn, a wound for a wound, a bruise for a bruise . . ."[53] It would appear that this command is purely retributive: Whatever harm is inflicted on the other, the law requires that equal harm be done to the perpetrator. However, Jewish sages have never interpreted this literally. That is, hands, teeth, and eyes were not torn out as recompense for injuries to those body parts. Instead, the sages have argued that the law should not be applied literally but should remain literally harsh in order to communicate the need for the perpetrator to seriously contemplate the severity of the damage inflicted. But neither could the slate be wiped clean by mere monetary restitution—though it was mandated.[54] In addition, the perpetrator was expected to beg for forgiveness from the victim and perform rites of repentance before God.[55]

   49. Lev 19:10.
   50. Lev 25:35.
   51. Ps 12:5.
   52. Amos 4:1.
   53. Exod 21:24–25.
   54. See the *Jerusalem Talmud*: "One who injures another is liable to pay compensation for that injury due to five types of indemnity. He must pay for damage, for pain, for medical costs, for loss of livelihood and for humiliation. How is payment for damages assessed? . . . [T]he court views the injured party as though he were a slave being sold in a slave market and the court appraises how much he was worth before the injury and how much he is worth after the injury. The difference between the two sums is the amount one must pay for causing damage . . ." (*Jerusalem Talmud*:y.Bik.83b–84a). See also Maimonides, "Rules of Repentance" in *Mishneh Torah*. Maimonides lists fifteen different ways to repent.
   55. The process of repentance, literally "return" in Hebrew, is called *Teshuva*. There

CHAPTER 4   JESUS' GOD

Like all ancient peoples, the Israelites believed that offering gifts, that is, sacrifices, to Yahweh was one of the primary ways to redress the harm caused by injuring others, since whatever harm was caused to others was also a breach of Israel's relationship with Yahweh. While the Israelites were carrying the ark of the covenant with them as they traveled to Canaan, they established sites for sacrifice in various locations, such as Shiloh or Gilgal. But when at last a magnificent temple in Jerusalem was constructed to provide permanent housing for the ark, all sacrificial rites took place there. The location for sacrifices was an outdoor altar, tended by priests, directly in front of the darkened chamber that held the ark—the presence of the living God.

Sacrificial offerings (called *Korban*, or *Qorbanot*) were likely part of the religious expression of the Israelites long before Yahweh gave them Torah. Maimonides, the great medieval Jewish sage, opined that the laws of Torah that governed sacrifice were actually an accommodation to even more ancient pre-existing practices.[56] At no time, however, did Israel believe that sacrifices could manipulate Yahweh in any way. This made Jewish sacrificial practices distinctly different from those of the pagan cultures that surrounded Israel—including the Greek and Roman cultures of Jesus' day. In the Greco-Roman culture, the various gods were capricious, selfish deities, whose intentions could be influenced by making sacrifices, including human sacrifices. In contrast, the functions served by Jewish sacrificial offerings were thanksgiving, restoration, or atonement.

In his mercy, Yahweh provided for ritual observances in order to restore broken relationships. Depending upon the nature of the sin, these offerings were in thanksgiving, in restoration of relationship, or in atonement. The first type of offering was that of the fruits of the land. Jews were required to bring these offerings to Jerusalem three times per year as part of the three harvest pilgrimages of Passover (*Pesach*), Weeks or Pentecost (*Shavuot*), and Tabernacles or Booths (*Sukkot*). The offerings were entirely eaten by family and friends, thus strengthening the bonds of the community. Peace offerings were a second type of sacrifice, with the purpose of bringing the believer into closer communion with God. These could be thanks offerings for God's bounty and mercy; the Hebrew term for this type of sacrifice derives from the root for *Shalom,* meaning

---

are many ways to perform *Teshuva*, from praying for forgiveness, to doing good deeds, to teaching others not to sin. See Ben Avraham, *The Gates of Repentance*.

56. See Ben Avraham, *Qorbanot: Sacrifices and Offerings*.

"peace" or "wholeness." Third, there were burnt offerings, whose name in Hebrew, *Olah*, comes from the same root as the word "ascension." The animal sacrificed would be completely consumed by fire on the altar, so that the smoke of the sacrifice would ascend to Yahweh. Burnt offerings thus represented the complete surrender of the offeror to God. Finally, the fourth form of ritual comprised sin offerings intended as an atonement for error and as a token of the desire to be reconciled with God.

Chapter 5   Jesus' Witness

OUR MEDIA-DRIVEN CULTURE OVERWHELMS us with bad news on a daily basis—and there is certainly always plenty of bad news to go around. Still, Jesus and his followers had it much, much worse. They were largely subsistence farmers, taxed into poverty by Jewish leaders appointed by Rome, forced to live in a culture whose values radically departed from the faith of their ancestors, largely illiterate, and deprived of any sense of national identity. It was within this life of desperation that Jesus was raised and within which, as an adult, he preached the "good news." But what was this good news Jesus was supposed to have taught and proclaimed?

Hope for a New World

According to Luke's Gospel, Jesus first proclaimed the good news when he returned to his hometown after his time in retreat: "The Spirit of the Lord is upon me, because he has anointed me to bring good news to the poor. He has sent me to proclaim release to the captives and recovery of sight to the blind, to let the oppressed go free; to proclaim the year of the Lord's favor."[1] Then Jesus said, "Today this scripture has been fulfilled in your hearing." Here, Jesus quotes a passage from the prophet Isaiah, who was speaking of his own role as a prophet to reassure Israel that there would be an end to the exile in Babylon and a restoration to God's favor and blessing. If we look back at Jesus' ministry, though, we see that—if Jesus believed that his message of good news would *literally* set Israel free, end oppression, reduce

---

1. Luke 4:8.

poverty, and heal all of those who were blind, all in Jesus' lifetime—he was sorely mistaken. He must have had something else in mind. In any event, the folks in Jesus' hometown were not particularly interested in what Jesus was proclaiming; they were incensed that the man they knew as Joseph's son had the gall to proclaim that he had been anointed as a prophet to proclaim this good news. So, the question remains: What did Jesus mean by "good news," and what do Jesus' actions during his lifetime reveal about it?

The short answer is that, for Jesus, the good news was that God was acting in a new way to at last bring the ancient promises of social justice and freedom to fulfillment. Everything Jesus did was intended to serve as a foretaste of what lay in the future. Because the future held the promise of human transformation, Jesus healed. Because the future held the promise of socio-economic equity, Jesus told stories about the fate of the wealthy. Because the future held the promise of an end to oppression of all kinds, Jesus confronted the Jewish power elite and then turned over the tables of the temple money changers. Jesus called this future the "kingdom of God"—a time fast approaching when God's law of love rather than human self-interest would finally reign.

Jesus used a series of parables to communicate what the kingdom of God is and how it comes about. In one of his most famous parables, Jesus described a sower who casts seed on various types of soil—rocky, arid, thorny, and good soil. The sower is obviously God, and the point Jesus was making was that the right conditions must prevail in order for the kingdom of God to begin to grow.[2] The various conditions of the soil are the various obstacles in place that prevent us from hoping not only that the kingdom can come but also that we will all play a role in bringing it about. In the parable of the mustard seed, in which a huge tree can grow from the tiniest of seeds, Jesus was pointing out that a future glorious possibility is already hidden in the present moment and requires only the smallest step to start its growth. In the same vein, Jesus described the possibility of heaven on earth as yeast that, in tiny amounts, leavens three measures of flour.[3] Two additional parables, one about a merchant in search of fine pearls and one about a person in search of treasure, describe the preciousness and surpassing value of the reign of God and how our discovery of its possibility brings ultimate joy.[4]

2. Matt 13:23.
3. Matt 13:33.
4. Matt 13:24–30, 47–50.

Moreover, two additional parables make the point that the coming of the kingdom will coexist for a time with the reality of human sin. One parable tells the tale of a householder who discovers that there are weeds in his field as well as the good seed he sowed, and a second tells of a fisherman who caught "fish of every kind" and, only when the net was full, threw out the bad ones.[5] These parables reassure us that, although it may appear that evildoers are not being brought to justice during our own lives, God will reward the righteous at the appointed time.[6]

The Way

A critical part of Jesus' prophecy about heaven on earth is his teaching about *how* to make the new world come into being. In fact, before Christianity coalesced into a state-sponsored religion, Christianity was known as "the way," that is, a way for human beings to learn to embody the vision and so bring it to fruition. Jesus was certainly not the first to come up with the idea of a path or way to holiness. The same concept, *dharma*, is one of the foundations of Buddhism and, in Jesus' own tradition, there was a set of rules and practices derived from both Torah and scribal extrapolations of Torah that is called *halakhah*, or "the path that one walks." It is also worth recalling that Judaism, then as today, is not a system of beliefs so much as it is a "way" of living.

In order to understand what Jesus had in mind, it is important to understand what people in biblical times meant by the "heart" because this is the term used throughout scripture to denote not only a person's physical center but also the seat of a person's emotional/intellectual/moral capacities. The heart was *the* central organ, the one that moved the rest of the body. So, for example, eating not only strengthened the body but also the heart.[7] The understanding that the heart can open to the experience of the divine lies as deeply in Jewish prophecy and psalmody as other key themes such as testing, restoration, and blessing. Moses promised the Israelites that Yahweh would circumcise their "hearts" and the hearts of their descendants ". . . so that you will love the Lord your God, with all your heart and with all your soul, in order that you may live."[8] So central to Judaism is this promise that

---

5. Matt 13:24–30, 47–50.
6. Matt 13:43.
7. Waltke, *Heart*.
8. Deut 30:6.

it is recited ritually in the *shema*, the core profession of Judaism: "Hear, O Israel! The Lord is our God, the Lord is one! You shall love the Lord your God with all your heart, and with all your soul, and with all of your might."[9] God knows the secrets of our hearts: "Man looks at the outward appearance," says Samuel, "but the Lord looks at the heart."[10] Also important to an understanding of Jesus' vision is the meaning of "repent." Repent does not mean "confess your sins" in either Hebrew or Greek. The term in Hebrew is *teshuva*, which literally means "return," the belief being that sin drives people astray from their natural destiny to live in God's presence by obeying God's laws. The term in Greek is *metanoia*, meaning to change one's heart or change the direction of one's life or sense of purpose.

Because the state of our hearts is affected by our moral disposition, which is "devious above all else,"[11] and because Israel's history was one of consistently falling away from Torah, God made a new covenant with Israel. This new covenant ". . . will not be like the covenant that I made with [your] ancestors when I took them out of the land of Egypt . . . a covenant that they broke . . . But this is the covenant that I will make with the house of Israel: I will put my law within them, and I will write it on their hearts . . . No longer shall they teach one another, 'Know the Lord', for they shall all know me . . .".[12]

Thus, the good news was not only that a new world is in the offing but that God's desire for us is that we can bring it about as a response to God's transformation of our hearts. The supreme good news is that we can actually learn *to love as God loves* and even *embody* the love that underlies sacred scripture. According to Mark's Gospel, Jesus inaugurated his ministry by announcing: "The time is fulfilled, and the kingdom of God has come near; repent, and believe in the good news."[13] To paraphrase, Jesus was saying, God is about to take redemptive action! Let your hearts be open to hear and believe in this good news!

Because the synoptic gospel writers did not understand what the good news really was—that it is a vision, yes, but also *a road map to attain the vision*—they did not look for the "narrow path"[14] to the conversion of the

---

9. Based on Deut 6:4–5.
10. 1 Sam 16:7.
11. Jer 17:8.
12. Jer 31: 32–34.
13. Mark 1:14–15.
14. See Matt 7:13-14: ". . . But small is the gate and narrow the road that leads to life,

heart among the extant lore about Jesus. Indeed, it is a distinctive feature of the way Jesus is presented in the gospels that there is no description of the "way"—that is, of the process leading to conversion—in contrast to, say, the *dharma* in Buddhism or the "Five Pillars of Islam." Nonetheless, it strains belief that Jesus, one of the greatest spiritual teachers the world has known, did not teach a path of human transformation that at least bears some similarities to the paths outlined by other great teachers.

That path, in very brief summary, starts with some kind of awakening. The awakening opens up a kind of flow between the newly awakened "soul" and the Divine, in which the Divine invites the soul to experience an ever-deepening communion. The soul experiences a comforting sense of being known and also in some sense "knowing" the Divine.[15] As the sense of loving communion deepens, the soul experiences a process of surrender of the so-called "false self," or the self constructed to navigate the world, and awakening of the "true self," or the self that more authentically reflects Divine love.[16] The end of the journey has various names in various traditions, such as *nirvana* in Buddhism and Oneness of Being/Oneness of Appearance in Islam.[17] In Christianity, the term used is "mystical union"—that is, a sense in which one's false self is wholly surrendered and the true self fully realized within the Divine.

By contrast, the gospel writers chose to construct a loose biographical framework culminating in the last three days of Jesus' life, piecing the extant oral lore together in catchy groups to support that structure. The result is a patchwork with little thematic consistency or progression of ideas. Even to call these passages in the Gospels of Matthew and Luke a "sermon" is a misnomer, since sermons normally contain one or two clear messages that are introduced, developed, and concluded, whereas the Sermon on the Mount is actually a sequence of random groupings, called "pericopes." To add insult to injury, Luke organized his pericopes in a different sequence than Matthew. By way of example, both the Sermons in Matthew and Luke start with the so-called Beatitudes—a recitation of all of the ways God in the future will comfort those who suffer in the present moment. Here is an example from Matthew of the sequence of pericopes that follows the Beatitudes:

---

and only a few find it."

15. See Anonymous, *The Cloud of Unknowing*.
16. Keating, *Invitation to Love*, 144 (purification of the unconscious).
17. See Muhummad, *The Concept of Mystical Union*.

> Rejoice and be glad, for your reward is great in heaven, for in the same way they persecuted the prophets who were before you. You are the salt of the earth; but if salt has lost its taste, how can its saltiness be restored? ... You are the light of the world. A city built on a hill cannot be hid ... Do not think that I have come to abolish the law or the prophets; I have come not to abolish but to fulfill ... .[18]

Here is the same sequence from Luke's gospel:

> Woe to you when all speak well of you, for that is what their ancestors did to the false prophets. But I say to you that listen, Love your enemies, do good to those who hate you ... If anyone strikes you on the cheek, offer the other also ... .[19]

Considering that Jesus' core message was the advent of God's reign on earth, it seemed astonishing to me that there is no teaching in the gospels about what the conversion process necessary to its advent entails. The gospels tell us that, after his baptism, Jesus was driven out to the wilderness, where he underwent his own process of surrendering his false self—that is, grappling with his egoic needs for security, power, and renown.[20] Does it make sense that he would have withheld what he knew from his own experience from his closest disciples? It makes more sense to assume that Jesus did teach a "way" to his disciples—if only because that is how Christianity was known in the early years—than that he did not. Might that "way" be found within the teachings in the Sermon on the Mount? What would happen

---

18. Matt 5:13.

19. Luke 6:27 *et seq.*

20. Thomas Merton writes, "The self-proclaimed autonomy of the false self is an illusion: every one of us is shadowed by an illusory person: a false self. This is the man I want myself to be but who cannot exist because God does not know anything about him ... My false and private self is the one who wants to exist outside the reach of God's will and God's love—outside of reality and outside of life. And such a self cannot help but be an illusion ... For most people in the world, there is no greater subjective reality than this false self of theirs, which cannot exist. A life devoted to the cult of this shadow is what is called a life of sin ... Thus I use up my life in the desire for pleasures and the thirst for experiences, for power, honor, knowledge and love, to clothe this false self." He goes on: "Eventually and inevitably that which is too awful to think about finally happens. Death reveals in us that eventually tomorrow is today and that we have run out of time. We discover by force of death that [t]here is no substance under the things with which I am clothed. I am hollow, and my structure of pleasure and ambitions has no foundation ... And, now that they are gone, there will be nothing left of me but my own nakedness and emptiness and hollowness, to tell me that I am my own mistake." Thomas Merton, *New Seeds of Contemplation*, 34–35.

if the various pericopes in the Sermon were rearranged? Might the "way" emerge? After all, I reasoned, there is nothing in principle preventing me from rearranging them in any way that made sense. What I discovered is that not only is it possible to reconstruct the Sermon so that it very clearly outlines the "way" of surrender of the heart but also that the Lord's Prayer, which traditionally comes at the end of the Sermon, is an almost perfect encapsulation of the "way" Jesus laid out.

Following, then, is a rearrangement of the Sermon on the Mount as it appears in Matthew's Gospel:

1. Jesus casts the vision: "Strive first for the kingdom of God and His righteousness, and all these things will be given to you as well." (Matt 6:33)

2. A fundamental choice must first be made, however: ". . . Store up for yourselves treasures in heaven . . . for where your treasure is, there your heart will be also." (Matt 6:19–21)

3. Making the choice involves honesty about what you really value: "No one can serve two masters . . . You cannot serve God and wealth." (Matt 6:24)

4. Know that God has already made you good enough to change the world: "You are the light of the world. A city built on a hill cannot be hid . . ." (Matt 14–16)

5. Be aware that fear for yourself and judgment of others will stop your progress: "Do not worry about your life, what you will eat or what you will drink . . . Your heavenly Father knows that you need all these things . . . Do not judge, so you may not be judged . . . Why do you see the speck in your neighbor's eye, but do not notice the log in your own eye?" (Matt 5:25, 32; Matt 7:1–5)

6. Engage in a "fearless moral inventory" so that you can learn to treat others with compassion: "If your right eye causes you to sin, tear it out and throw it away . . . it is better for you to lose one of your members than for your whole body to go into hell." (Matt 6:29)

7. Understand that conversion is a soul-deep process and not a superficial display: ". . . Whenever you fast, do not look dismal, like the hypocrites . . . But when you fast, put oil on your head and wash your face, so that your fasting may be seen not be others but by your Father who is in secret . . ." (Matt 6:16)

8. Conversion of the heart comes about also by *acting* consistent with what you believe: "Everyone ... who hears these words of mine and acts on them will be like a wise man who built his house on a rock ... Not everyone who says to me 'Lord, Lord' will enter the kingdom of heaven, but only the one who does the will of my Father in heaven." (Matt 7:24, 26)

9. Learn to pray by honestly sharing what is in your heart with God: "When you are praying, do not heap up empty phrases as the gentiles do; for they think that they will be heard because of their many words. Your Father knows what you need before you ask Him." (Matt 6:7)

10. To sum it all up: Remember that God is Father to all and that God is infinitely holy. Choose to align your will with God's desire for you. To that end, trust your needs completely to God and seek constant forgiveness for the ways in which you succumb to fear and judgment. Ask only that God help you to see these temptations for what they are. In other words, "Our Father in Heaven, hallowed be your name. Your kingdom come. Your will be done on earth as it is in heaven. Give us this day our daily bread. Forgive us our debts, as we also have forgiven our debtors. And do not bring us to the time of trial, but rescue us from the evil one. Amen." (Matt 6:9–13)

11. The rewards for choosing the "way" of the heart are a sense of abundance, goodness, blessedness, and discernment: "Is life not more than food, and the body more than clothing ... The eye is the lamp of the body. So, if your eye is healthy, your whole body will be full of light." (Matt 5:11–12; 6:12) "For if you forgive others their trespasses, your heavenly Father will also forgive you ..." (Matt 6:14) "Beware of false prophets, who come to you in sheep's clothing but inwardly are ravenous wolves." (Matt 7:15)

12. The "way" is the fulfillment of both the law and the prophets: "Do not think that I have come to abolish the law or the prophets; I have come not to abolish but to fulfill." (Matt 5:17)

If this message sounds familiar, it's because it closely resembles the Twelve-Step sequence of Alcoholics Anonymous and related recovery programs. I must not be the only person who has mined the Sermon on the Mount for timeless wisdom about human transformation.

CHAPTER 5 JESUS' WITNESS

Mercy in a Culture of Law

What about Jesus' teachings taken as a whole? Could they guide me to a more complete sense of Jesus' sense of identity and mission? One of the signature characteristics of Matthew's account of Jesus' Sermon on the Mount is the number of times Jesus says: "You have heard it said . . . but I say to you . . ." Since Matthew's audience is believed to have been potential Jewish converts to the new faith, it makes sense that Matthew would refer to normative Judaism as the point of departure for describing the ways in which Jesus' teachings presented something new. But how would I figure out what would have been new teachings for Jesus' listeners unless I understood the old teachings? Because . . . wouldn't it be Jesus' new teachings that formed the basis for his new vision for God's kingdom on earth?

In Jesus' time, the only legitimate moral authority was the Torah, the foundational laws God had given to Moses, and the only legitimate interpreters of the Torah were, first, the Pharisees and Sadducees, or the temple elite, and, second, those who copied the law, or the scribes. Torah, as previously noted, consisted of the Ten Commandments and the 613 laws contained in the book of Leviticus. The Levitical laws primarily focus on the role of the priests, but they also order, with great specificity, the routines of daily living, such as how and what to eat, with whom to socialize, and how to treat land and animals.

Beyond these sets of foundational law, however, another body of law developed over time, called *mishna*. Mishna is the accumulation of law developed by learned men whose task was to decide how to apply Torah to new questions that naturally arose over time. Among the Jewish cultic hierarchy in Jesus' time, the Sadducees generally took the most conservative approach to applying Torah, while the Pharisees perpetuated the vibrant tradition of mishna. The kinds of questions that concerned the Pharisees involved how the foundational laws—especially the Levitical laws—should be applied to everyday living. If, for example, Torah teaches that it is unlawful to work on the Sabbath, does that mean that a housewife can't tidy up the house? Does it apply only to intentional work for monetary gain, as opposed to, say, doing a *mitzvot* (a good deed) for someone else? To criticize these laws was to take on the norms of an entire culture, as well as those authorized to regulate it.

Central to Jewish understanding of Torah is that its highest fulfillment is love. This affirmation forms the holiest of prayers, the *shema*: "Hear, O Israel: The Lord is our God, the Lord alone. You shall love the Lord your

God with all your heart, and with all your soul, and with all your might,"[21] and in the law: "You shall not take vengeance . . . on any of your people but you shall love your neighbor as yourself . . ."[22] In line with this tradition, Jesus taught that every application of the law was to be guided by these two laws of love—love of God who always shows mercy, and love of self and others who are always in need of mercy. One of the most moving stories of this approach to Torah is that of a scribe who asked Jesus which law was the greatest of them all. Jesus responded, quoting the above passages, whereupon the scribe exclaimed: "You are right, Teacher; you have truly said that 'he [God] is one, and besides him there is no other'; and 'to love him with all the heart, and with all the understanding, and with all the strength' and 'to love one's neighbor as oneself'—this is much more important than all whole burnt offerings and sacrifices." Seeing that he answered wisely, Jesus said to him, "You are not far from the kingdom of God."[23]

The imperative of love, however, leaves open the question of how the law should be applied to particular situations so as to fulfill the law's highest purpose. This is the issue that most often put Jesus in the Pharisees' cross-hairs. Jesus challenged the Pharisees' application of the law on at least two grounds. The first was that the Pharisees sought to expand the meaning of the operative legal terms in a particular law beyond the intent of that law. Jesus used the context of Sabbath observance to make this point. The third of the Ten Commandments requires that the Sabbath be kept "holy." This commandment had long been interpreted to exclude any activity other than rest, walking, and study. Harvesting crops was forbidden because it was considered work. When the Pharisees spotted Jesus and his disciples walking in a grain field and plucking heads of grain because they were hungry, they accused Jesus of allowing his disciples to "harvest" the grain, thus extending the definition of "harvest" to include "plucking." Jesus responded by reminding the Pharisees that the high priest had allowed King David to feed his starving troops with the "bread of Presence," even though it was reserved for priests alone and then only after the priests had undergone proper sanctification procedures.[24] The high priest, in questioning David, had learned that David's troops had abstained from sex for three days and that the vessels to be used had been sanctified and

21. Deut 6:4–9.
22. Lev 19:18; cf. Mark 12:30–31.
23. Mark 12:32–34.
24. See 1 Sam 21:1–6.

so reasoned that the intent of the law—preserving the holiness of the bread of Presence—could also be fulfilled in this instance.

What Jesus was pointing out was that, whereas expanding the law by the Davidic high priest actually enhanced the underlying imperative (i.e., ensuring that the bread would be sanctified), the plucking of grain on the Sabbath to feed hunger in no way furthered the imperative of resting on the Sabbath. The only possible conclusion was that the Pharisees were seeking to enforce the law not because it furthered the purpose of the law but just because they could. That is why Jesus called his disciples "guiltless" and made it clear that the issue was not whether "plucking" comes within the definition of "harvesting" but rather the pointless exercise of power for its own sake: "But if you had known what this means, 'I desire mercy and not sacrifice', you would not have condemned the guiltless. For the Son of Man is lord of the sabbath."[25] This is a not-so-gentle reminder that, in trying to expand the law—not to serve the highest law of love but to reinforce their power—the Pharisees would have to answer to God, who, after all, had created the law. This latter point is captured in the story of the difference between a "good shepherd" and a "hired hand." The good shepherd owns the sheep and the sheep know the difference between the good shepherd and anyone else who tries to lead them. Moreover, the good shepherd is willing to sacrifice to the point of giving up his own life when the wolf comes to attack. The hired hands seek only their own advantage and, when the wolf comes to call, make a fast exit over the fence.

Jesus' second challenge to the way in which the Pharisees were applying the law was their tendency to apply the law strictly. Under this theory, it doesn't matter whether, in the individual case, considerations of mercy prevail over the value of enforcing the law whenever, in the particular situation, the law clearly applies. For example, in Matthew's Gospel, the Pharisees and the scribes questioned Jesus about why his disciples were "breaking the tradition of the elders" by not washing their hands before eating. In typical fashion, Jesus countered with another question: "And why do you break the commandment of God for the sake of your tradition? For God said, 'Honor your father and mother', and, 'Whoever speaks evil of father or mother must surely die.' But you say that whoever tells father or mother, 'Whatever support you might have had from me is given to God,' then that person need not honor their father."[26] Jesus was criticizing

25. Matt 12:7–8.
26. Matt 15:3–7.

the Pharisees for allowing people to make *korban* as a substitute for supporting their parents, thereby violating the much more important Fourth Commandment. This is the essence of hypocrisy: that the Pharisees were insisting on strictly applying the relatively minor table laws, while simultaneously not hesitating to encourage others to violate the foundational law of love of the Fourth Commandment.

Jesus was not just critical of the manner in which the Pharisees applied the law, however; he also took issue with the purity laws themselves. As noted previously, these laws (mostly found in Leviticus) classify things and actions as either "clean" or "unclean." They are not just minor rules or regulations but are foundational to Jewish identity as a people sanctified by God as God's holy nation. Many people today are familiar with the kosher laws that consider animals with only cloven hoofs or that only chew the cud impure, so that the person consuming them also becomes defiled. But the purity laws extended to every aspect of living, from table fellowship to various conditions, such as menstruation, spilled semen, various types of skin eruptions, and the skin of lepers. All uncleanness was regarded as sinful, even though no moral failing was associated with it. Most types of impurity were viewed as merely a temporary state that could be absolved through isolation from the community and/or specific cleansing rituals. However, some kinds of uncleanness, like leprosy, made the victim "ritually unclean" and required absolution from a priest if the victim was to rejoin the community.

Jesus did not take issue with all of the purity laws, perhaps seeing that the purpose of the laws as a whole was to separate Jews from evil.[27] So, it is noteworthy that Jesus was selective in the purity laws with which he took issue. The first grouping with which he took issue comprised the laws of table and table fellowship. Table fellowship formed the center of social life in Jewish communities. To be excluded from table fellowship meant exclusion from the heart of community and family life. Jesus openly flouted some of these laws as a way of emphasizing inner holiness over right observance. For example, regarding the requirement of ritualized hand washing before meals, Jesus said,

> Listen and understand: it is not what goes into the mouth that defiles a person, but it is what comes out of the mouth that defiles . . . Do you not see that whatever goes into the mouth enters the

---

27. See Douglas, *Purity and Danger*, 41–57; Wenham, *The Theology of Unclean Food*, 6–15; Silber, *Jewish Dietary Laws*, 12–16.

stomach, and goes out into the sewer? But what comes out of the mouth proceeds from the heart, and this is what defiles. For out of the heart come evil intentions, murder, adultery, fornication, theft, false witness, slander. These are what defile a person, but to eat with unwashed hands does not defile.[28]

With respect to the table fellowship rule that a righteous Jew would only break bread with the undefiled, Jesus' practice was to invite the socially outcast to join him.[29] Thus, when Jesus welcomed tax collectors and others who were in a state of sinfulness to his table, the Pharisees rightly questioned him: What kind of Jew would invite defilement? Jesus' reply was, "Those who are well have no need of a physician, but those who are sick; I have come to call not the righteous but sinners."[30]

Jesus was therefore setting an example of gracious restoration to the community of anyone with the humility to acknowledge their need for forgiveness—even those who had so grossly betrayed the community by collecting taxes for the Roman oppressors. For Jesus, the only legitimate distinction between "clean" and "unclean" was the distinction between a humble heart and a heart convinced of its own superior righteousness. Jesus made this point personal to the Pharisees by telling a story about a Pharisee and a tax collector, both of whom had gone to the temple to pray. The Pharisee's prayer was one of gratitude that he would surely be justified by God because he devoutly observed Torah. The tax collector's prayer was one of desperate acknowledgement of his sin. Of the two, Jesus pointed out, only the humble sinner would be justified.[31]

While Jesus used some of the table fellowship purity laws to make the point that mere observance of the law does not necessarily change the heart, he outright rejected the purity laws that marginalized anyone on purely categorical grounds. People with leprosy, non-Jews, or Samaritans, for example, were deemed presumptively unclean, not because they had willfully sinned, but only because they happened to fit into a category. The most well-known story illustrating Jesus' take on these laws is certainly that

---

28. Matt 15:10–20.

29. See Blomberg, "Jesus, Sinners, and Table Fellowship," 35, for an analysis of the many instances of Jesus' table inclusivity determining their historical authenticity.

30. Mark 2:16–17.

31. Luke 18:9–14. "Justified" means that God has removed the guilt and penalty for the sin and has restored the sinner to "righteousness" (or right relationship) before God.

of the Good Samaritan.[32] By way of background, ritual purity laws barred both priests and Levites, experts in the law, from touching a dying or a dead body. For priests, such defilement required seven days of cleansing; for Levites, who were temple helpers, the cleansing rituals were somewhat less strict. Samaritans lived in Samaria, a territory that lay between Judea and Galilee. They claimed to be the descendants of the northern Jewish tribes that had long ago disappeared from the historical record. They, too, claimed to be Jews, even though their temple was in Samaria and not Judea, and even though their ritual practices differed from those of their southern neighbors.[33] The southern tribes, of which Jesus and his followers were members, considered the Samaritans enemies, with an enmity going back centuries. Jesus' story unfolds as follows: A man—presumably a Jewish man—was attacked by robbers on the road to Jericho (in Judea) and was left for dead. Three people were traveling on the road at the same time: a priest, a Levite, and a Samaritan. The priest and Levite passed by without offering assistance. But the Samaritan stopped, tended to the man's wounds, took him to a nearby inn, and paid the bill.

There are a couple of subtexts in this story, one of which is the same issue Jesus criticized regarding the table fellowship laws: The very people who were especially called to be agents of God's mercy believed that strict observance of the law—and preserving their own purity—was more important than acting with compassion. On a broader note, Jesus also used the laws associated with ritual purity to make the point that laws that permanently exclude others from the community on the basis of mere externals may simultaneously be excluding those who have a true sense of God's will, and that "enemies can prove to be good neighbors, that compassion knows no bounds, and that judging people on the basis of their religion or ethnicity will leave us dying in a ditch."[34]

So ingrained was the importance of preserving Jewish culture through categorical purity laws that even Jesus had to learn differently. As noted earlier, Jewish law considered anyone who was not Jewish to be unclean by definition because they ate unclean food and associated with unclean people. Since the time of the return from Babylonian exile, this most radical

---

32. See Luke 10:29–37.

33. The Samaritans believed that they were "original" Jews in that they had not been transported to Babylon but stayed in Israel, while the two southern tribes, Benjamin and Judah, were taken into exile.

34. Levine, "The Many Faces", 23.

CHAPTER 5   JESUS' WITNESS

form of ethnic exclusion between Jews and gentiles had been perceived by Jews as essential to their identity and survival as God's people.[35] So it is noteworthy that both Mark's and Matthew's Gospels tell of Jesus' encounter with a Syro-Phoenician woman as he traveled to regions north of Israel.[36] The woman pleaded with Jesus to exorcize a demon from her daughter, but, to her dismay, Jesus not only refused, explaining that his ministry was for the Jews alone, but also called her a "dog." Undeterred, the woman countered that even dogs were fed table scraps by the Jews. Jesus was so moved by the woman's humble faith that he immediately healed the woman's daughter. Jesus' action thus becomes not only a commentary on the righteousness of non-Jews but, like the story of the Good Samaritan, a broader statement about the triumph of compassion over prejudice.

The capstone of this approach to Torah is vividly illustrated in Jesus' parable of the "prodigal son." Jesus tells of a landowner who had two sons. The younger son asked his father to give him his inheritance in advance and then took off for parts unknown, where he squandered his inheritance in dissolute living. The elder son stayed home, dutifully serving his father and caring for the household and property. The younger son was forced to seek employment as a hired hand and ended up feeding pigs—the most unclean of animals. But then the young son "came to himself" and remembered that his father's hired hands at least had decent food to eat. So, he decided to return home, ask for forgiveness, and beg for employment as one of his father's hired hands. But, to his astonishment, he learned that his father had been searching the horizon for him every day since the son's departure. Before the son could beg forgiveness, his father ran out to him, put his arms around him, and kissed him. Then, the father arranged for the son to be clothed in the finest clothes and to be the featured guest at a lavish celebration, exclaiming, ". . . [T]his son of mine was dead and is alive again; he was lost and is found!"[37]

This is a story about a faithful and dutiful son and an errant and degraded son—or, in other terms, a Torah-abiding son and an unclean sinner who flouted the sacred laws. Strict application of Torah would

---

35. Indeed, one of the first tasks of Ezra, the new religious leader of a restored Israel following the Babylonian exile was to develop a new Holiness code that forbade intermarriage and required those who had not been exiled and who had married non-Jewish women to divorce them. Intermarriage was seen as polluting the purity of the seed and thus imperiling Israel's sense of identity and holiness. See Ezra 9 *et seq.*

36. Matt 15:21–28; Mark 7:24–30.

37. Luke 15:24.

call for the younger son to be deemed unclean and to have to undergo a purification process in order to be readmitted to the community. Even then, he would at least be required to atone to his father for the loss of the squandered inheritance. Instead, the father offered open-hearted forgiveness with no strings attached.

As a whole, then, Jesus told stories that were bold declarations of the true meaning of Torah: mercy over strict interpretation of the law, unqualified forgiveness in the face of repentance, and purity and wholeness of heart over strict observance of the law. But Jesus' stories also illuminated the unfitness of the religious leaders to interpret and apply the law—particularly regarding their exploitation of Torah to affirm their own sense of importance and their power base. It's no wonder that Jesus' fate was the same as that of anyone who speaks truth to power, then as now.

Love as a Fulfillment of Torah

Love is our deepest need and our most ardent desire. Being able to receive and give love allows for the fullest expression of our human nature. Our tragic human condition is that most of us can only partially experience love, and the love we do experience—whether romantic, parent-child, or friendship—is subject to hurt, loss, or diminishment. Nonetheless, Jewish sacred scripture teaches that God is always extending God's self to us as love, no matter how far we stray from God's will for us, and that God's love is faithful, eternal, just, and merciful. For Jesus, God's love was also experienced in a personal and intimate way, so much so that it claimed him completely. Jesus believed that his unique vocation was to embody God's love fully, and to demonstrate, through the manner in which he lived a human life, what God intended human lives to be. In particular, Jesus' life highlights four aspects of divine love—sacrifice, hope, mercy, and healing—that, if practiced, would bring God's reign to earth.

You would think, then, that the gospels would talk about love—its texture and its source. But they don't—with one exception. John's Gospel is unlike the other gospels in many respects (e.g., it only loosely attempts a chronology of the events leading to the crucifixion and resurrection), most notably because it focuses on the saving power of a loving relationship with Jesus as the "Son of God" ("But these are written so that you may believe that Jesus is the Christ, the Son of God, and that by believing, you may have life in his name"[38]). So, in what ways does John's gospel open up Jesus' message of love?

The first and most obvious answer is that, in John's gospel, Jesus explicitly identifies himself as embodying (i.e., "incarnating") God's love for humankind. Readers no longer need to play a guessing game about who Jesus was, as we do in the synoptics. In John's gospel, Jesus says: "I am the truth, and the way, and the life. No one comes to the Father except through me."[39] The "truth" is that God is love;[40] the "way" is that we are to love each other as Jesus loved his disciples;[41] the "life" is eternal but also experienced in the now;[42] and, if we entrust our lives to Jesus and his way of love, God can transform us into God's own son or daughter. While the kingdom of God is the major theme and the source of the good news in the synoptic gospels, the theme in John's gospel is Jesus as the source of eternal life ("I have testimony weightier than John [the Baptist]. For the works that the Father has given me to finish—the very works that I am doing—testify that the Father has sent me"[43]) and the good news is that we, like Jesus, can be one with God and with each other. In effect, John's gospel is a segue to the Sermon on the Mount. While the Sermon on the Mount is all about *how* to begin a process of transformation, John's gospel is an exposition of *what* love looks like in practical reality.

Sacrifice

Theologians have speculated that Jesus' willing sacrifice of himself was actually the seal of a new covenant between God and his people, one that recalled the release from slavery in Egypt and the great exodus toward the promised land. The argument is that—just as God ordered the Jews to kill an unblemished lamb and sprinkle its blood on their doorposts, so that when God killed all of the Egyptian firstborn males, God would know to "pass over" the Jewish households—God offered Jesus as a sacrificial lamb to save those who accept him as their savior. Today, in every mass celebrated, the priest intones "Christ, our Passover, is sacrificed for us. Let us eat the

38. John 20:31.
39. John 14:6.
40. 1 John 4:8.
41. John 2–12.
42. John 3:15–16, 6:47.
43. John 5:36.

feast."[44] We have already noted that this idea would never have occurred to Jesus as a devout Jew. For him, the Passover was the definitive, salvific event for Israel, with no possibility or need for a repeat performance. Moreover, Jesus *could not* have held this view. Anyone who has attended a Jewish seder knows that it is a feast designed to *recall* the hardships of the Jewish people, their slavery in Egypt in particular, and to *celebrate* the goodness and favor of the God who hears the cries of his captive chosen. The blood of the sacrificial lamb was not meant as an atonement for sin (rather, Yom Kippur is the day especially set aside for reflection and atonement) but rather as a sign to alert Yahweh to "pass over" the houses of the Jewish slaves when he slaughtered the firstborn sons of the Egyptians. Because of this sign, Yahweh would know *to spare and to save* the chosen people from destruction.

Additionally, the Passover seder follows the common practice in Judaism of offering a blessing both before and after a meal, the first a blessing on the "bringing out" of nourishment and the second a benediction on being nourished, called the *birchat ha-motsi*. This blessing reads, in part:

> Blessed are you, Lord our God, King of the universe, who, in His goodness, provides sustenance for the entire world with grace, with kindness, and with mercy. He gives food to all flesh, for His kindness is everlasting. Through his great goodness to us continuously we do not lack food . . . For He, benevolent God, provides nourishment and sustenance for all . . . His creatures whom He has created . . .

This blessing always involves taking a small amount of bread and/or a small amount of wine and saying the blessing over it. The blessing after the Passover seder is similar but adds a special recognition of the blessing of the Passover. Thus, this theory of so-called "substitutionary atonement" is not only incorrect as a theological matter but also flies directly in the face of God's new revelation of Godself through Jesus as personal savior, tender parent, and eternal source of love and peace. Yet, Jesus did willingly sacrifice his life, and so we must ask, to what end?

Jesus was clearly aware that he had sufficiently threatened the wealthy Jewish clerical hierarchy and that it was likely that he would be accused of blasphemy, for which the punishment was death by stoning. There were a number of ways to commit blasphemy—from speaking God's name, to outright cursing God, to engaging in deliberate and flagrant sin. Jesus

---

44. This belief is what caused gentiles who heard about the Jesus cult to believe that Christians were cannibals.

committed none of these offenses, and the Sanhedrin knew it. But there were two events that, taken together, gave the Sanhedrin legitimate cause to try Jesus for blasphemy under Jewish law. The first is that, while in the temple precincts, Jesus turned the tables of the temple money changers over, scattering both coins and the animals destined for sacrifice, and then predicted that the temple would soon fall. All four gospels include this event, attesting to its historical truth; the synoptic gospels even place this story near the end of Jesus' ministry, as if to demonstrate that it was this action that precipitated Jesus' arrest.

The second event that led to a charge of blasphemy was Jesus' response to the high priest's question: "Are you the Messiah, the Son of the Blessed One?"[45] Jesus' answer was to quote a passage from the book of Daniel predicting that the "Son of Man," who sits at God's "right hand" (i.e., holding a special place of honor before God) would come "with the clouds of heaven."[46] Although Jesus never claimed that he was the Jewish Messiah, he often called himself a "son of man." So, his veiled prediction that the temple would be destroyed, together with a self-reference that paralleled the coming of a celestial being, not only threatened the livelihood and power of the Sanhedrin but also suggested (to the high priest, at least) that Jesus was claiming to be a kind of god, of which there could only be one. And, to the extent that others believed that Jesus was the Messiah, he was obviously an imposter because he bore no resemblance to the Davidic Messiah that scripture described.

So, Jesus knew what was coming, even though he prayed to the point of sweating blood that God would offer him some other alternative to the horrible death that awaited. As a Jew, he could draw no comfort from thoughts of heavenly bliss, since Jews did not believe in heaven except as a place where God and the heavenly court resided. The best that Jesus could hope for was to rest in the bosom of Abraham with his ancestors.[47]

Some scholars have suggested that solidarity with the plight of Jesus' followers—particularly his empathy with their poverty and subjugation—lies at the heart of his sacrifice.[48] But archeological evidence from

---

45. Mark 14:61.

46. Dan 7:13.

47. Cf. Luke 16:22, the parable of the rich man and a beggar, Lazarus, who each die. Lazarus is carried by angels to the bosom of Abraham, while the rich man can only see Lazarus across an impassable chasm in hell.

48. See, e.g., Reiser, *Jesus in Solidarity*, 180; Borg, *Jesus*, 274.

Capernaum, where Jesus taught and where Peter and his family lived, as well as evidence from the villages in and around Nazareth, reveal that the inhabitants, though poor to modern eyes, lived modestly but comfortably off trade and agricultural products.[49] Moreover, Jews had lived side by side with the officials and soldiers of multiple invading empires, most of which allowed the Jews to continue to worship their god and live according to their god's laws. Other scholars see Jesus' acceptance of death as an act of redemptive solidarity with the human condition: that God was acting through Jesus' death and ensuing resurrection to demonstrate not only that God is "with us" in our suffering but also that God will transform our suffering into a redemptive purpose. From Jesus' perspective, this argument is obviously specious, since, when he accepted the reality of crucifixion, he did not know that God would raise him from death. After all, his final cry from the cross was "my God, my God, why have you forsaken me?"[50] If the consoling words Jesus offered to the thief dying next to him are to be believed, Jesus believed that he would go to "paradise" after his death rather than being resurrected from the grave.[51]

More fundamentally, though, both of these theories of a redemptive cross confuse solidarity with love. Jesus could have remained in complete solidarity with his vision and his followers and still have decided to go underground. But he could not flee and still be faithful to the God he loved and trusted and whom Jesus knew loved him and had entrusted him with a unique mission. Jesus was not the only one to experience this love; if the sacred texts were reduced to a single assurance, it would be that God is *always faithful to God's promises*—despite slavery, infidelity, exile, famine, flood, and pestilence—and *always acts redemptively* toward those whom God loves. Hadn't God demanded that Abraham sacrifice his beloved son, Isaac, and wasn't it Abraham's trust in God that, even as he lashed his son to the altar of sacrifice, caused an eleventh hour reprieve? *Jesus' choice to die was the only possible option if he was to be faithful to the God who had given him the vision he proclaimed.* Also, and not secondarily, the vision God entrusted to Jesus promised shalom *for others*—a value higher than the life of any single person. This willingness to sacrifice, for the sake of God's greater vision or for the sake of the greater common good, is implicit in the *shema* and is the very essence of the Jewish understanding of God's love. Thus,

---

49. Magness, *Stone and Dung*, 35.
50. Mark 15:34.
51. Cf. Matt 27:45–54.

Jesus accepted the relative insignificance of his own life compared with the hope of fulfillment of God's vision for the Jewish people. If that meant that Jesus, like Moses, would never see the promised land, it was enough to know that God would be faithful.

To teach the sacrificial imperative of this kind of love to his disciples, Jesus fashioned a new ritual that he, true to form, refashioned from existing practices in order to imbue it with new meaning. Known as the "last supper," it took place—depending upon which gospel you read—either as an add-on to the seder meal held on the Day of Passover (the synoptic gospels) or following a ritual of foot washing held on the Day of Preparation for the Passover (John's gospel). In either case, all the gospels agree that the new ritual was held on the eve of the day that Jesus was crucified. But what is important here is that Jesus deliberately chose to go to Jerusalem at the time of Passover. After the meal, when the *birchat ha-mason* would have been said, Jesus took a loaf of bread, "said thanks, . . . broke it and said: 'This is my body that is for you. Do this in remembrance of me.' In the same way he took the cup also, after supper, saying, 'This cup is the new covenant in my blood. Do this, as often as you drink it, in remembrance of me.'"[52] Jesus' message was one of thanksgiving for God's nourishing love, first and foremost. Secondarily, it was a message announcing a new covenant between God and his people—no longer a hierarchical one in which the lord of the house graciously shares his largesse with his servants but a communitarian one in which the lord befriends his servants, considers them beloved sons and daughters, and shares himself completely with them. Thus is the circle of love complete, as those who have shared and those who have received experience the good news of what love is and how it grows: ". . . [L]ove one another as I have loved you. No one has greater love than this, to lay down one's life for one's friends. You are my friends if you do what I command you."[53]

An additional noteworthy feature of the last supper/foot washing is what Jesus *did not* say. He did not say: "Believe this" in order to be saved; or "eat this" to remember me. He said "*Do* this" to remember me. That is, "feed each other as I have fed you." Or, in John's gospel, "wash each other's

---

52. This is a quotation from St. Paul's first letter to the Corinthians, the earliest Christian writings we have (1 Cor 11:23–26). In it, Paul also says that he received the wording of this rite directly from (the risen) Jesus himself.

53. John 15:12–14.

feet as I have washed yours." "For I have set you an example, that you should do as I have done to you."[54]

Hope

Jesus began his Sermon on the Mount with nine affirmations of hope. He promised his listeners that, if they were weighed down by life's hardships at the present time, they would soon see the advent of God's new kingdom come to earth. Likewise, if they were being persecuted because of their belief in the coming of God's kingdom, they would be sustained in knowing that they would soon experience it for themselves. If they were mourning, they would soon be comforted; if they were humble, they would experience the full glory of the kingdom; if they earnestly sought the coming of the kingdom, their desire for it would be satisfied; if they pursued shalom, they would receive God's shalom; and, if their hearts were pure, they would experience God for themselves. It is difficult to imagine a more hopeful vision of what might be possible for human beings. So, in order to turn vision into reality, Jesus called twelve men to live a monastic life, to travel with him, and to learn "the way" of consenting to God's love and to the conversion of their hearts, which would, in turn, bring the kingdom of God into living reality. These men would be the first generation of those who would proclaim Jesus' vision of hope for humankind and teach the path to its fulfillment.

Scholars have tended to confuse this message of hope grounded in human possibility with the apocalyptic eschatology of Jesus' age. "Apocalyptic" is derived from a Greek term, meaning "to uncover" or to "lay bare," and "eschatology" refers to end time events. Together, these terms predict a time when all the evil in the world would finally be exposed and then utterly destroyed by God in an earth-shaking natural cataclysm. All creation would be wiped clean so as to be ready for the coming of the Son of Man and his new reign of justice, peace, and prosperity. All this was predicted in the book of Daniel and quoted chapter and verse by Jesus when the high priest demanded to know whether he was the Messiah.[55]

Scholars wrongly conflate the apocalyptic prophecies contained in the synoptic gospels with Jesus' mission to establish God's kingdom on earth, perhaps because there is a lack of understanding about what Jesus actually meant by the "kingdom of God." But, while it is easy to see that the

---

54. John 13:15.

55. See, e.g., Matt 24–25, Mark 13, and Luke 21, quoting Dan 7.

apocalyptic vision contained in the book of Daniel fits neatly into Jesus' self-references as "a son of man" and his predictions about the coming of the kingdom of God, the kingdom of God and the coming of a new age are different in two key aspects. The first is that the coming of end times is about the hope that, even if justice is beyond the reach of the present, justice will at last prevail over oppression and exploitation at some point in the future. The kingdom Jesus predicted, on the other hand, was to be realized within the present state of political and historical affairs. Evidence of this is found in the fact that Jesus' disciples thought Jesus was going to be the new king and fought over which disciple would be given the most power in the new kingdom[56] and in the fact that the Romans identified Jesus as "king of the Jews" in a sign posted directly above his head as he hung dying. Jesus' resurrection only served to reignite this understanding of the imminence of the kingdom Jesus had predicted:

> But we do not want you to be uninformed, brothers and sisters, about those who have died, so that you may not grieve as others do who have no hope. For since we believe that Jesus died and rose again, even so, through Jesus, God will bring with him those who have died.[57]

Second, the visions of the apocalypse all involve wiping out large segments of the human race before an age of justice and prosperity could arrive.[58] In Jesus' kingdom, however, sinners (including foreign oppressors) were forgiven, loved, and reunited with the community. Both visions obviously offer enormous hope, but the coming of the kingdom of God would so change human hearts that an apocalyptic vision of the eschaton would no longer be necessary.

Mercy

John's gospel tells the story of Jesus and a woman caught in adultery.[59] Jesus was teaching in the temple precincts, when some scribes and Pharisees brought him a woman who had been caught in the act of adultery. Under Jewish law, the punishment for adultery was to be stoned to death. Aware

---

56. See Mark 10:35–45.
57. 1 Thess 4:13–17.
58. See, e.g., Mark 13; Matt 24.
59. John 8:1–11.

that the religious officials were trying to trap him into disavowing the sacred law, Jesus at first refused to answer. When he finally did answer, it was not to make a pronouncement on the law but rather to ask the accusers to consider whether they had, at any point, committed a sin. Since it was nearly impossible to live daily life without becoming defiled by unclean things, Jesus was making the point that none of us are free enough of sin to impartially judge another. And then, as the woman's accusers walked away, Jesus—as if to make the pronouncement on the law that they had baited him with—told the woman that he would not judge her either, instead admonishing her to change her ways. We are left with little doubt that this formula of mercy, together with a command to take a more righteous path, was the beginning of a new life for the unnamed woman.

John's Gospel, more than any of the others, depicts Jesus as God's eternal Son, disguised as a first-century rabbi. If we accept this version of Jesus' identity, the message of the above story is that God's judgment is first and foremost merciful, and, since it is merciful, it is also redemptive. God's self-revelation to Moses was, "The Lord, the Lord, a God merciful and gracious, slow to anger, and abounding in steadfast love and faithfulness . . . forgiving iniquity and transgression and sin, yet by no means clearing the guilty . . ."[60] If we accept the version of Jesus' identity that has been developed here, the message is that people have no right to accuse another of wrongdoing until they have looked fearlessly into their own heart—that is, from a stance of humility, not moral superiority. If this is done, the only honest response is one of mercy. Jesus' understanding of the dialectic of judgment and mercy is thus rich with the same predisposition toward mercy that characterizes God in the sacred texts but with a clear deepening in understanding of our predisposition to judge rather than to show mercy. It is not because human nature inevitably leads us to stray from God's will, as manifested in God's laws, that God rightly judges us and then, relenting, acts mercifully and sets us back on the right path. Rather, it is that our ignorance of our own real motives makes us reflexively judgmental and that we prefer to place ourselves in a morally superior position over others rather than do the harder and more painful work of self-scrutiny. Jesus therefore offers an alternative to the cycle of inevitable sin/punishment/mercy/restoration by opening up another, more redemptive possibility: that it is within our power to choose whether our default will be mercy rather than judgment.

60. Exod 34:6.

CHAPTER 5   JESUS' WITNESS

Forgiveness

Forgiveness is different from pardon. Pardon is an act showing mercy by remitting just punishment or releasing a person from the penalty for an offense. Forgiveness can also result in the remission of a debt or a sin, but the driving force behind it is a change of heart from feeling resentment or the need for revenge. It is a willingness to restore a relationship that was altered by sin. The Jewish sacred texts tend to muddy this distinction, however, by using the terms interchangeably or using different terms altogether to mean one or the other. For example, when King David ordered Uriah the Hittite to be killed so that David could take Bathsheba as his wife, the text tells us that the "Lord has *put away* your sin."[61] When Israel rebelled against God during the long journey to the promised land, Moses begged God not to disinherit them or strike them down with illness. God responded: "I do *forgive*, just as you have asked; nevertheless—as I live, and as all the earth shall be filled with the glory of the Lord—none of the people who have seen my glory and the signs that I did in Egypt and in the wilderness, and yet have tested me these ten times and have not obeyed my voice, shall see the land that I swore to give to their ancestors; none of those who despised me shall see it."[62] "I am He who *blots out* your transgressions for my own sake, and I will *not remember* your sins," writes the prophet Isaiah.[63] And the prophet Micah writes, "Who is a God like you, *pardoning* iniquity and *passing over* the transgression of the remnant of your possession?"[64]

Despite the conflation and confusion of terms in the sacred texts, Jewish law in actual practice was more focused on "pardon" than "forgiveness." We have seen previously that sin or wrongdoing in Jewish thought is as much a sin against God as it is against others, and that expiation of the sin could only be granted by God. The early belief was that sin was a malefic force that adheres to human beings, such that only the interposition of a stronger divine force could cleanse or purify the sinner.[65] All sin required a three-part atonement process involving making things right with God through the prescribed rituals; confessing one's sin and performing acts of contrition, such as fasting and otherwise humbling

61. 2 Sam 12:13.
62. Num 20–23.
63. Isa 43:25.
64. Mic 7:18.
65. Jewish Virtual Library, "Forgiveness."

oneself; resolving not to sin again; and making restitution for any harm caused. Once this process was complete, the sinner could be certain that ". . . as the heavens are high above the earth, so is [God's] mercy great upon those who fear him. As far as the east is from the west, so far has he removed our sins from us."[66] On the other hand, while God, in God's mercy, does not "remember" the sin, God does not condone it, nor does God spare the offender the consequences of transgression.[67]

What we see in Jesus is forgiveness, not just pardon. Forgiveness is so central to Jesus' message about the conversion of the heart that it forms the core of the Lord's prayer: "Forgive us our sins as we forgive those who sin against us."[68] While this command is a contingent one (i.e., God forgives us to the extent that we forgive others), it places all parties on the same footing with each other and with God in much the same way as the *shema*'s requirement that we treat others as we would be treated. All parties share a presumptive dignity, dependent only on their willingness to forgive or to love. So vital is forgiveness to the coming of God's kingdom that, when Peter asks Jesus whether he should forgive someone who wronged him seven times, Jesus replies, No! Seventy times seven![69] and then tells a story about a king who wanted to settle the debts owed to him by his slaves. The king first called for a man who owed him a huge sum of money and, when the man could not pay it, the king ordered all of the slave's "possessions," including his wife and children, to be sold to satisfy the debt. The slave pleaded for mercy, and the king forgave him the entire debt. Soon after, the slave met up with another slave who owed the first slave a small sum. This second slave also pleaded for mercy, but the first slave—who had been so richly forgiven—refused to forgive the debt and cast the indebted slave into prison until he could pay the amount owed. When all of this was reported back to the king, the king summoned the slave and asked him, "Should you not have had mercy on your fellow slave, as I had mercy on you?" Jesus concludes, "So my heavenly Father will also do to every one of you, if you do not forgive your brother or sister from your heart."[70]

Thus, for Jesus, heart forgiveness is made possible through the experience of, first, recognizing the need for forgiveness; and, second, accepting

66. Ps 103:11–13.
67. See, e.g., Isa 43:23; Num 14:18.
68. Matt 6:12, Luke 11:4.
69. Matt 18:22; Luke 17:14.
70. Matt 18:23–35.

CHAPTER 5   JESUS' WITNESS

the reality that God has not only pardoned the sin itself but, like the father of the prodigal son, is waiting to welcome the prodigal back and to restore the lost relationship to its former loving mutuality.

For Jesus, forgiveness was instinctive. He forgave his executioners in the very midst of his agony ("Forgive them for they do not know what they are doing"[71]) and with deep compassion for the sin that lies most deeply in the human condition: that we can be so caught up in the banality of systemic cruelty that we actually come to believe that we are acting righteously.[72] We can imagine that, at some point, Jesus' executioners would come to realize their unintentional complicity in the death of an innocent man. But we can also imagine that they would remember the words that would save them from self-hatred and restore them to the sense of wholeness before God.

Healing

For us, disease is a misfortune resulting from an interplay of identifiable components—viruses or bacteria, socio-economic degradation, and environmental factors, for example. In Jesus' culture, however, illness was seen as a punishment—for either personal sin or sin committed by one's parents. Thus, we see that Jesus' disciples asked him, after he had healed a man born blind, "Rabbi, who sinned, this man or his parents, that he was born blind?"[73] to which Jesus' response was, "Neither this man nor his parents sinned; he was born blind so that God's works might be revealed in him."[74]

The actual cause of all afflictions was believed to be the work of malicious demons who inhabited an unseen world and preyed upon anyone who had, because of sin, brought the demons on themselves. The only way an afflicted person could be cured was through the intervention of a divine being more powerful than the forces of darkness. To make this point, Matthew tells the story of the healing of the paralytic, in which Jesus says, "Take heart, son; your sins are forgiven." Matthew continues, "Then some of the scribes said to themselves, 'This man is blaspheming.' But Jesus, perceiving their thoughts, said, 'Why do you think evil in your hearts? For which is easier, to say, 'Your sins are forgiven' or to say, 'Stand up and walk?'"[75] For

---

71. Luke 23:34.
72. See Arendt, *Eichmann in Jerusalem*.
73. John 9:2.
74. John 9:3.
75. Matt 9:2–5.

Jesus and the scribes, there was no practical difference between forgiving sin and healing. What the scribes took issue with was that Jesus forgave the paralytic—since only God, through the priests, could forgive sins—rather than simply ordering him to stand up and walk.

Despite the prevalence of these beliefs about healing, there was considerable nuance in what "healing" actually was and how healing occurred. The gospels use three different terms to describe "healing"—*sozo*, *therapeuo*, and *iaomai*—but they do not have interchangeable meanings. Each term emphasizes one or two kinds of healings over others. For example, *sozo* means to save, protect from danger, or be restored in spirit, soul, and body,[76] as in the following passages:

> She [Mary] will bear a son, and you are to name him Jesus [or "Yeshua," "one who rescues or delivers"], for he will *save* [*sozo*] his people from their sins.[77]
>
> Then suddenly a woman who had been suffering from hemorrhages for twelve years came up behind him and touched his cloak, for she said to herself, "If I just touch his cloak, I will be *made well* [*sozo*]."[78]
>
> [Those at the foot of the cross mocked Jesus, saying] He *saved* others; he cannot *save* [*sozo*] himself. He is the King of Israel; let him come down from the cross now, and we will believe in him.[79]

Sozo is translated as "saving" 120 of the times it appears in the King James Version of the Bible and as "healing" only three times.[80] But the examples above reveal that "saving" could mean deliverance from sin, which might or might not include curing an illness ("he will save his people from their sins"); a holistic healing of both a physical ailment and the need for restoration to a "whole" life ("I will be made well"); or a physical rescue from certain death ("he cannot save himself"). *Sozo*, then, encompasses healing in the broadest sense of the term: as a rescue or deliverance from external harm in the literal sense and, in the spiritual sense, as a restoration to wholeness.

It is in this regard that *sozo* is related to *shalom*. As noted previously, in addition to being a greeting of peace, *shalom* is one of the many names

---

76. Kittel and Friedrich, *Theological Dictionary*.
77. Matt 1:21.
78. Matt 9:21.
79. Matt 27:42.
80. Strong, *Concordance*.

for God. A *shalom* blessing is found on the oldest fragment of biblical text: "The Lord bless you and keep you. The Lord make his face to shine upon you and be gracious unto you. The Lord lift up his countenance upon you and grant you *shalom*."[81] For our present purposes, *shalom* derives from *shalem*, meaning "whole or complete." Adam and Eve were created in and for *shalom*, and humankind would have continued to experience eternal *shalom* but for its tendency to disobey God's commandments and laws. *Shalom* is preserved in Jewish law by proscriptions such as forbidding the planting of two different kinds of seeds in a single field, using only complete stones for an altar, not mixing different kinds of materials in weaving a garment, and not blending different kinds of animals.[82] Since healing is, by definition, a restoration to a former wholeness, both of the individual and of the community that previously marginalized the individual, Jesus often dismissed those he healed with the words, "Your faith has healed you. Go in *shalom*";[83] "*Shalom* I leave you, my *shalom* I give to you";[84] "While they were saying these things, he himself stood in their midst and said *shalom* to you";[85] and "Grace and *shalom* be with you."[86]

Therapeuo, a subset of *sozo*, is a second term for "healing." It refers to treating the sick or curing through various measures—that is, therapeutics—but it can also include miraculous healings and casting out demons.[87] In the passage about the hemorrhaging woman cited above, the gospel writer noted that [the woman] ". . . had spent all she had on physicians [but] no one could *cure* her (*therapeuo*) . . . [But Jesus] said to her: 'Daughter, your faith has *made you well* (*sozo*); go in *shalom*.'"[88] *Therapeuo* was almost uniformly translated as "curing" (38 of the 48 times it appears in the KJV), in passages such as,

---

81. Num 6:24–26.
82. Lev 19:19; Deut 25:11.
83. Mark 5:34; Luke 7:50, 8:48.
84. John 14:27.
85. Luke 24:36.
86. This phrase opens most of Paul's letters to the new churches.
87. To be recalled is that casting out demons did not necessarily mean exorcisms, since demons were believed to be the primary cause of all types of illness.
88. Luke 8:43, 48.

> But now more than ever the word about Jesus spread abroad; many crowds would gather to hear him and to *be cured* (*therapeuo*) of their diseases . . .[89]
>
> And he *cured* [*therapeuo*] many who were sick with various diseases, and cast out many demons . . .[90]
>
> And Jesus rebuked the demon, and it came out of him, and the boy was *cured* [*therapeuo*] instantly.[91]

When the term *therapeuo* was used by the gospel writers, it most often meant the physical curing of specific diseases.

Finally, the gospel writers used *iaomai* to describe the release of divine healing power in instant, miraculous healings often coupled with the casting out of demons.[92] This kind of healing was primarily physical, but it could also include healing of the heart, which, it will be recalled, referred to the center of a person's mind or character. *Iaomai* is used thirty-two times by the gospel writers collectively to describe Jesus' healings; in twenty-eight of those times, it is translated as "heal." *Iaomai* may be regarded as a subset of *therapeuo* because it covers the same type and range of healing but adds the dimensions of being instantaneous and associated with specific prerequisites such as acknowledgement of sin, the laying on of hands, or a profession of faith. Occasionally, both terms are used in the same passage:

> They came to hear him and *to be healed* [*iaomai*] of their diseases; and those who were troubled with unclean spirits were *cured* [*therapeuo*]. And all the crowd were trying to touch him, for power came out from him and *healed* [*iaomai*] all of them.[93]
>
> But the crowds were aware of this and followed Him; and welcoming them, He began speaking to them about the kingdom of God and *kai tous chreian echontas therapeias iato* [literally, "and those need having healing (*therapeias*), He was healing (*iato*)"].[94]

To summarize, all the terms the gospel writers used to describe Jesus' ministry to the afflicted denote "healing" in some form or another. *Sozos* is the term used most often to describe what Jesus did, and, when it is used,

---

89. Luke 5:15.
90. Mark 1:34.
91. Matt 17:18.
92. Kittel and Friedrich, *Theological Dictionary*.
93. Luke 6:18.
94. Luke 9:11.

it is translated as "saving" or "salvation." This makes sense, since sin was the precondition that invited illness, and healing or curing an illness required a "saving" act of divine will. Moreover, the prevalence of *sozos* over other kinds of healing is consistent with the aspiration of *shalem*—that the natural state of everything God created is "perfect" or "whole" when it is restored to the fullest expression of itself. "Healing" in the broadest sense included both a physical curing and a spiritual healing of whatever stood in the way of one's fullest expression of one's human nature.

The story of the ten lepers illustrates this point. Ten lepers were standing by the side of the road, begging to be healed. Jesus ordered all of them to go to the temple and obtain the forgiveness of a priest, as the law required, and, on the way to the temple, all ten were healed. One of the ten, a Samaritan, when he realized he had been healed (*iato*), turned back,

> . . . praising God with a loud voice. He prostrated himself at Jesus' feet and thanked him . . . Then Jesus asked, "Were not ten made clean [*ekathanristhesan*]? But the other nine, where are they? Was none of them found to return and give praise to God except this foreigner?" Then he said to him, 'Get up and go your way; your faith has made you well [*sozos*].[95]

Although Jesus was honored as a wise teacher, he was renowned for his ability to heal. Yet, as astonishing as Jesus' miracles of healing were, they would have seemed somewhat less unprecedented in Jesus' time. The prophets Elijah and Elisha were also known to have had healing power,[96] so the mere fact that Jesus healed did not set him apart. Moreover, in ancient times, every healing—especially of serious illness or disability—would have been regarded as miraculous. This is the framework within which we can now turn our attention to the three aspects of Jesus' healing ministry that were unprecedented. Of paramount importance, as suggested above, was that Jesus' ministry was focused on healing—not prophesying, not building a movement, not seeking the overthrow of the ruling elite.[97] To the extent that Christianity teaches that Jesus was both human and divine at the same time, it is extraordinarily significant that, of all of the ways God could have manifested Godself in Jesus, God chose healing.

---

95. Luke 17:11–19.

96. See, e.g., 2 Kings 4:20–37 (Elisha, described in the text as "the man from God," raises a sick boy from the dead).

97. Quite the opposite—the entire theme of the Gospel of Mark is the "messianic secret" that the disciples were forbidden to proclaim.

Moreover, these were not healings of simply annoying or even debilitating conditions; they were healings of devastating, life-altering conditions, such as paralysis, deafness, blindness, or leprosy. It is conceivable that the gospel writers included so many stories of healing not because such events dominated Jesus' agenda but because the gospel writers were trying to prove that Jesus was the very Messiah mentioned by the prophet Isaiah.[98] Given that the few existing accounts of Jesus' life written by non-believers remember him foremost as a healer, however, it seems incontestable that this is what he was primarily known for.

To be emphasized is that Jesus' healings were ends in themselves, not (as some have argued) performed as a "sign" of something else, whether as a vindication of God's power over evil, to lend credibility to the healer, or to mark the coming of the kingdom of God. Jesus did not use people's suffering to make a statement about something else. Rather, as the story of the woman healed of hemorrhaging by merely touching the fringes of Jesus' garment shows, healing flowed out from Jesus' very being as *living proof of God's presence among God's people and of God's compassion, lavish and limitless*. It is in this sense that Jesus' explanation of why he healed the man born blind must be understood—not that God makes people ill so that God can demonstrate his power over sin, but that God acts with boundless compassion over even the most apparently hopeless circumstances of our lives.

Yet, while Jesus' intention in healing was not to use suffering people as proof of his or God's power, it is equally clear from the previous discussion on the Sermon on the Mount that the coming of the reign of God on earth is intimately associated with healing. If it is God's desire that human beings fulfill the highest purpose for which they were created, to learn to love as God loves, it is also manifestly clear that this kind of loving only arises from a deep wholeness. Indeed, once even a tiny taste of wholeness is experienced, it has a power of its own to bring wholeness to others. Jesus made this point in the parable of the mustard seed. The mustard plant was believed to have healing properties because of its pungent taste and fiery effect.[99] Even though it is tiny, once it takes root, its growth and proliferation are unstoppable.

---

98. See the book of Isaiah: "Then the eyes of the blind shall be opened, and ears of the deaf unstopped; then the lame shall leap like a deer, and the tongue of the speechless sing for joy . . ." (Isa 35:5–6).

99. See Pliny, *Natural History*, 528–29.

CHAPTER 5   JESUS' WITNESS

The second unprecedented aspect of Jesus' healing ministry is that it was sacrificial. Jesus was willing to put himself at risk in order to relieve suffering, as in his healing of lepers, for example. Lepers suffered not only from a life-destroying skin disease but also from complete shunning, forced to stay off to the side of the roads and to wear bells to signal their presence. When a man with leprosy came to Jesus, begging Jesus to "make him clean," Jesus *touched* him, cleansing the man of leprosy and defiling himself in the process. Moreover, there is no doubt that Jesus' healing ministry was exhausting, both physically and spiritually. Nearly as often as the gospel stories narrate stories of healing, they describe times when Jesus got into a boat to flee the hectoring crowds or withdrew to deserted places to rest and pray.[100]

The third aspect in which Jesus' healing was unprecedented has already been hinted at: It was deeply personal—intimate, often physical, interaction between Jesus as a loving physician and a person in need. Previously, God's saving/healing action had manifested itself largely in the fulfillment of God's promises to his holy people: "Do not fear, you worm Jacob, you insect Israel! I will help you, says the Lord; your Redeemer is the Holy One of Israel . . . I will open rivers on the bare heights, and fountains in the midst of the valleys; I will make the wilderness a pool of water, and the dry land springs of water. I will put in the wilderness the cedar, the acacia, the myrtle, and the olive . . ."[101] But, when Jesus healed, it was personal, just as Jesus' relationship with the Source of love was personal—an affirmation that each and every person's life was precious and worth saving.

What do the unique aspects of Jesus' relationship to his culture, his God, and his vision of God's reign on earth, taken together, tell us about what Jesus actually taught? Overall, we can say that Jesus saw his mission as that of bringing his own experience of God as a tender and loving father to the members of his own community as their father, too. A new community, a new "kingdom," would be formed around the vision of God as Father of all and as a living, healing Presence. The bedrock of these teachings was, of course, Judaism, which Jesus fully embraced. Indeed, Jesus' teachings *only* make sense within the context of Judaism. Yet, Jesus' vision of a new kingdom of God's reign on earth led him to confront the Jewish power brokers whom Jesus believed were blocking the unfolding of his vision. Jesus thus confronted the Pharisees, the enforcers of the purity laws, with the claim

---

100. See Luke 4:42; 5:15–16.
101. Isa 41:14, 18–19.

that the laws were being used to shame and exclude rather than as means of sanctification. Even more radically, he invited the Sadducees and the priests—the temple power elite—to consider the possibility that the very people whose actions most offended the law might instead be the righteous ones in God's eyes. Jesus declared that God cares much more about purity of heart than right observance and, most startling, that *anyone* who shows Torah's values of mercy, compassion, and forgiveness stands on equal footing with Jews as children of God. He even challenged the exercise of judgment over others *by anyone and in any form* unless those exercising power had examined their own hearts from a stance of surrender and humility. Above all, Jesus taught about a God who was always searching for his people, whether they were clean or unclean; to whom the *shalom* of every single person mattered, no matter what human judgments had been made; and who eagerly waits to suspend all judgment, lavishing mercy on anyone with a humble heart. As a sign of this kind of love and in order to ensure that the new community would remember these teachings, Jesus established a new ritual that would bind them to each other in his "name."

So, what does this discussion say about whether and to what extent Jesus' teaching about the law departed from his culture? Of paramount significance is the fact that Jesus did not reject the law outright but used certain of the purity laws to emphasize the Torah's values of love and mercy. The criticisms he leveled at the Pharisees were never in derogation of Torah, nor of the importance of disciplines in religious life, nor even of the legitimacy of the cultic hierarchy of Judaism. Rather, Jesus took issue with the ways in which the Pharisees interpreted Torah for their own self-aggrandizement and applied it in ways inconsistent with its foundational principle of love and mercy. In this regard, and to the degree that a merciful application of Torah was essential to the welfare and restoration of the community as a whole, Jesus falls squarely within the Jewish prophetic tradition. Where Jesus departed from the prophetic tradition was in his total rejection of the purity laws that treated certain individuals—who fell into this category through no fault of their own—as non-persons. In the process, and as a result, Jesus was calling forth a new kind of community: one that observed the sacred laws but only as guided by the Torah's principle of love and forgiveness for all people, clean or unclean, who were willing to acknowledge their need for it.

This may not exactly sound like good news! But neither did Jesus promise an easy road, as he compared the path toward sanctification and

CHAPTER 5   JESUS' WITNESS

union with God to a gate into the city of Jerusalem called the "Eye of the Needle," a gate so narrow that travelers had to unload their camels in order to pass through. It is, however, profoundly good news to the "poor and the oppressed, the captives, and the blind"—the people Jesus told his townsfolk he had come to liberate—because their plight in life had forced them into humility and prevented them from being players in the ways of the world. These people did not have much baggage to unload, and yet they were being promised that their very suffering and marginalization was actually the source and wellspring of a life transformed by divine love.

This does not mean, as so many have argued, that Jesus' message was only about socio-economic justice, although that is the outcome when the hearts of an entire community are converted to the way of love. The good news Jesus preached and instructed his disciples to preach is that it is possible—but not easy—to create a transformed world in this life: a world that cares for the poor, the captives, the oppressed, and the blind. Jesus called this transformed world the "kingdom of heaven," or "heaven on earth." It is thus both a *vision* for humankind and also a *way* to attain the vision. It was, finally, Jesus' response to the perennial question of why a loving God condones suffering, whether socio-economic or otherwise.[102]

Having laid out the path to inner transformation, Jesus, in his teachings as a whole, took on the forces that worked to prevent people from following that path. What was truly novel—and scandalous—about Jesus' approach to the law was his unwillingness to restrict the *shemah's* requirement of treating one's neighbor as oneself to fellow Jews and thereby to exclude outsiders who might also be capable and worthy of compassion. The unmistakable message is that God cares first for purity of heart, and anyone who shows Torah's values of mercy, forgiveness, and compassion stands on equal footing with the Jews as children of God.

---

102. The awareness of human suffering, in death, loss, and disease, was what also compelled Siddhartha Gautama ("Buddha") to teach about how we can address and overcome our suffering. It is also based on compassion for self and for others. The primary difference between Jesus' and the Buddha's understanding was that Jesus believed in a living and personal God who was the source of all compassion, while the Buddha believed that everything is impermanent and changing.

Chapter 6   Beloved of God

JESUS WAS FIRST AND foremost a great spiritual teacher. He knew how to cast a vision; knew the human heart and its need for reassurance and hope; and spoke truthfully both about the challenges and the benefits of radical inner transformation. As we can see, Jesus' Sermon on the Mount was actually a sermon that any monastic would recognize as descriptive of the process of shedding the "false self" and rediscovering the God-created self. Jesus was also a mystic whose sense of identity as one with the Father originated in the events of his baptism and extended through the forty days Jesus himself underwent a process of transformation. He was not a prophet in the traditional sense, nor would he have been as effective a teacher if he had not been free to turn away from his vocation and had he not undergone the internal struggle that leads to transformation. In this sense, Jesus' identity and his mission are inseparable, so completely did he surrender to the will of the God he knew as "Abba."

Revolutionary

Jesus' teachings tell us a lot about what Jesus believed his mission to be. And, if these teachings were the sum of everything Jesus taught, Jesus would have been a reformer only. But Jesus was a revolutionary, announcing, in his Sermon on the Mount, a new vision of God, of God's dream for his people, and of the way in which it is possible to change the human heart so that God's kingdom might actually come. For Jesus, this was the true meaning of the Torah's imperative of love of self and love of neighbor: Love of self as God's own begets love of neighbor and thus God's reign on earth expresses itself as a community of neighbors.

Beloved of God

Thus, the gospels portray Jesus as a unique figure in the history of Judaism. The story of Jesus' uniqueness began with the manner of Jesus' summons, or call, at his baptism. As Jesus was being baptized by his cousin, John the Baptist, the heavens opened, a dove descended on Jesus' head, and the voice of God announced: "You are my son, the beloved; with you I am well pleased."[1] This experience of being in the presence of the Holy has a long heritage in the Hebrew scriptural descriptions of God's call to the very prophets Jesus most often quoted in his teachings. We are told, for example, that Isaiah's ministry began with a vision of God, sitting on a heavenly throne and attended by six seraphs, calling out, "Holy, holy, holy is the Lord of hosts; the whole earth is full of his glory." Isaiah cried out, "Woe is me! I am lost, for I am a man of unclean lips, and I live among a people of unclean lips; yet my eyes have seen the King, the Lord of hosts!" Then one of the seraphs flew toward Isaiah and touched his mouth with a live coal that had been taken from the altar. The Lord then asked, "Whom shall I send?" And Isaiah responded, "Here am I; send me!"[2]

Jeremiah's experience of vocation also began with an experience of the mysterious holiness of God, followed by a corresponding sense of utter unworthiness in the face of God's holiness and then a final assent and surrender to God's will. God told Jeremiah, ". . . Before I formed you in the womb I knew you, and before you were born I consecrated you; I appointed you a prophet to the nations." Jeremiah responded: "Ah, Lord God! Truly I do not know how to speak, for I am only a boy . . ." Then God touched Jeremiah's mouth with his hand, saying, "Now I have put my words in your mouth. See, today I appoint you over nations and over kingdoms to pluck up and to pull down, to destroy and to overthrow, to build and to plant."[3] Like Isaiah and Jeremiah, the prophet Ezekiel's ministry began with a vision of the likeness of God seated on a sapphire-like throne, surrounded by fire and splendor.

---

1. Mark 1:10–12.
2. Isa 6:3–8.
3. Jer 1:4–10.

> When I saw it [the throne], I fell on my face, and I heard the voice of someone speaking. He said to me, "O Son of Man, stand up on your feet and I will speak with you." And when he spoke with me, a spirit entered into me and set me on my feet; and I heard him speaking to me: "Son of Man, I am sending you to the people of Israel, to a nation of rebels . . ."[4]

At his baptism, Jesus experienced the same overwhelming presence of God and sense of call directed to him personally. But there are important differences between Jesus' call and the call to the earlier prophets. The first is a sense that God, in calling Jesus "my son," was initiating a new kind of relationship. God had not previously called any of Israel's prophets "my son" but, rather, used that title to refer only to the sonship of Israel:

> When Israel was a child, I loved him, and out of Egypt I called my son. The more I called them, the more they went from me . . . Yet it was I who taught Ephraim how to walk, I took them up in my arms; but they did not know that I healed them.[5]

Nor did any of the earlier prophets call God "Father," except in reference to God's relationship with Israel.[6] Nor did the three patriarchs of Israel with whom God had extended a personal covenant—Abraham, Moses, and David—refer to God as a father.[7]

It was Jesus' *response* to his experience of the call, however, that distinguishes him from the prophets. In calling Jesus "my son" at his baptism, God was extending to Jesus personally the same kind of tender and fatherly relationship from God's side that God had had with Israel. The gospels credibly bear witness to the fact that Jesus believed that God had singled him out for a new ministry based on his new identity as a child of God and not strictly as a prophet because Jesus called God *Abba*, an Aramaic title denoting special intimacy.[8] God would no longer maintain a distance by summoning the prophets to exhort God's beloved people to live righteously according to the law. God would now call a single person

---

4. Ezek 1:26—2:10.

5. Hosea 11:1–3.

6. See Miller, *God as Father*. Miller estimates that there are only about twenty references to God as "father" in the Old Testament, while there are dozens in the New Testament.

7. On the other hand, Yahweh is called "father" to Israel as a nation. See, e.g., Isa 64–66.

8. See Mark 14:36, Rom 8:15, Gal 4:6.

"beloved" and ask that person not only to *exemplify* how God's love transforms the human experience but also to teach others the path to a similar conversion.[9] As the Gospel of John describes it, Jesus was to be the Light of the world who, by his example and teaching, would lead others to becoming "the Light of the world."

Second, unlike the prophets, whose only option was to surrender to God's call, there is a sense in which Jesus was free *not* to accept this call—with no divine repercussions. By contrast, the prophet Jonah tried to flee from God's demand to go to Nineveh and tell its residents a message they did not want to hear. In his attempt to flee, Jonah was swallowed by a whale, but even there he was not out of God's reach, as the whale vomited him back onto shore, where Jonah finally realized that he was going to Nineveh whether he wanted to or not! Unlike Jonah, we do have the sense that Jesus could have ignored or denied God's call. We know from gospel references that Jesus was driven out to a wilderness area just after he was called and that he struggled with his own needs and temptations there, as being against the path God had put before him. He frequently returned to wilderness areas, seeking deeper and deeper discernment through private prayer. Perhaps most poignantly, Jesus fought with everything he had in the Garden of Gethsemane to be relieved of the fate that awaited him. In God's summons to Jesus, we see that, just as God is free, God honored Jesus' freedom.

A related aspect of this freedom is the sense that Jesus did not serve simply as a mouthpiece for God. All the prophets started or ended their various prophesies with the words, "Hear, O Israel," or "says the Lord," or "says your God," or "thus says the Lord of hosts," and they usually speak in the first person for God:

> Assemble yourselves and come together, draw near, you survivors of the nations! . . . Declare and present your case; let them take counsel together! Who told this long ago? Was it not I, the Lord? There is no god besides me, a righteous God and a Savior; there is no one besides me.[10]

---

9. To be clear, Jesus would never have imagined that God was his personal father. The God of Israel is far too mysterious to sustain any claim of human kinship. Rather, Jesus sought only to convey a new revelation of God who had always been *like* a merciful father, but who was now reaching out to human beings as individual persons rather than because they happen to be members of God's favored nation.

10. Isa 45:20–21.

But Jesus does not speak in these terms. Instead, he refers to himself and the vision he brings as the "fulfillment" of the earlier prophets, as *representing in himself*—in his vision for a new community and by the example of his life—what God had always promised God's people.

Thus, while the circumstances of Jesus' summons bore many resemblances to that of the ancient prophets—such as his complete internalization of God's Word, his many symbolic actions, and his reading of the times—his ministry cannot be wholly defined by a role. That Jesus most frequently referred to himself as "a son of man" suggests that his own self-understanding was that he was to serve as the fullest human expression of God's love for God's people. He did not stand outside his contemporaries as king, prophet, or priest; rather, he experienced life, with its temptations, uncertainties, blessings, and tragedies, as a human being. Indeed, it was surely this reality that allowed Jesus to speak so powerfully to a people longing for hope and to inspire them with a new vision of what their world might become. Yet, while Jesus was one of them, he was also convinced that God had given him a unique role: that of embodying God's love and, in the process, convincing others that this was the way to create a transforming community.

Therefore, the gospels build the case that, although Jesus resembled earlier prophets, he was a unique figure in the history of Judaism in that God had called him to actually manifest, in his very person—in his teachings and his life—what God's love looks like actualized in human life. His own experience of God's love for him was so intimate that he considered himself God's adopted figurative "son." From this relationship sprang Jesus' sense of mission: to cast a vision of what the world could be like if everyone's hearts were wholly transformed or "circumcised"; and to embody a heart wholly converted to love such that his followers might believe that the fulfillment of that vision was humanly possible.

Covenant Maker

Insofar as conclusions about Jesus' identity can be summarized at this point, it is important to recall that the very idea of an individual with a unique personal identity would have been alien to a first-century Jew. The very notion of an individual identity, apart from a confluence of one's relationships—with family, tribe, people, and history—would not have occurred to any first-century Jew. As evidence of this understanding,

Jesus chose the central communal rites of his people—baptism and table fellowship—through which to bear witness to the new revelation. Yet, because he had experienced Yahweh as personally as if Yahweh were his own father, Jesus modified these communal rites to reflect the fact that Yahweh was now seeking a new kind of relationship with his people. Baptism would no longer be a rite of cleansing and forgiveness of sins; it would now also, directly and individually, be the means of receiving the very Spirit of God. Table fellowship would not only be a ritual of thanksgiving for God's goodness and blessings; it would now also be a means of remembering what it had been like to actually experience God's love as the disciples had known it in Jesus.

Nevertheless, all four of the gospels were written in order to convince a particular audience that Jesus was the Davidic Messiah, a particular persona. This persona was the prophesied ancestor of David who would finally liberate Israel from oppression and usher in a new age of social justice, peace, and prosperity, enabling Israel to live into her destiny to be a light to the world. All three of the synoptic gospels make the issue of identity their core narrative secret: Will the disciples finally figure out who Jesus really is? Will they ever come to confess Jesus as the Messiah? These same gospel writers also appear to have shared the belief that the world was shortly coming to an end; some kind of cosmic apocalyptic event was in the offing; and Jesus the Messiah would come after these events, announced by the return of the prophet Elijah. Yet, every element of these beliefs is contradicted by what Jesus actually believed and taught and how he lived. Most obviously, Jesus preached peace and died forgiving his tormentors. The new kingdom that Jesus preached clearly had nothing to do with overthrowing Israel's enemies and restoring Israel to a time of justice, peace, and prosperity. And Jesus would have utterly rejected as blasphemy the belief that he was the "Son of God" in any sense other than that he aspired to be godly.

So, what other options do the gospels offer? One possibility is that Jesus was the cosmic "Son of Man." This personage more closely fits with both the eschatology of the age and the expectations of the early church that Jesus would soon return as a Messiah of a cosmic showdown. We have already noted that *the* Son of Man was a semi-heavenly being vividly described in the book of Daniel, whose arrival would be preceded by war against Israel and final victory by God. We have also noted that, in Mark's Gospel, the high priest asked Jesus, "Are you the Messiah, the Son of the Blessed One?" to which Jesus responded, "I am; and 'you will see the Son of

Man seated at the right hand of the Power' and 'coming with the clouds of heaven.'"[11] By this, Jesus might have meant: "I am the Messiah; the Messiah is the same personage as the 'Son of Man'; and I will return on clouds of heaven." Yet, just as there is no textual evidence for conflating the Davidic Messiah with the mystical "Son of Man" figure, there is no scriptural support for a belief that *any* kind of Messiah, either with a capital "M," or a lower case "m," was the same personage as the cosmic "Son of Man." They were always two separate expectations. On the other hand, Jesus could have meant, "I am the Messiah and I am prophesying that you will soon see another personage, the 'Son of Man,' coming on clouds of heaven." If we take Jesus at his word that he was the Messiah, he could only have meant it in the lower-case sense—that he was anointed to teach a new revelation of God in advance of the coming of the "Son of Man."

A third option is that Jesus was just a humble, lower-case "son of man." This kind of messiah was a prototypical human being, a son of man, or *ben-adam* in Hebrew, meaning a generic man, with special emphasis on a human's frailty or weakness in contrast to the Almighty.[12] Jesus is quoted as calling himself *a* "son of man" eighty times in the gospels. This was a messiah who experienced the heights and depths of human experience and who held a unique and unprecedented vision of what might be possible for human beings. When Jesus announced that the time for the beginning of his ministry had arrived, he quoted a passage from the prophet Isaiah in which Isaiah said, "The Spirit of the Lord is upon me, because he has anointed me . . . "[13] as if to say, "I am a messiah (an anointed one) and I will now be speaking God's truth." All in all, the image of Jesus as *a* son of man fits nicely with Jesus' core belief that God had commissioned him *in his humanity* to show his people what salvation really looked like.

We must conclude, therefore, that Jesus believed that he had been anointed by God to embody God's love. Recalling that "messiah" simply means "anointed one," Jesus believed that salvation for his people meant something entirely different than restoration to former days of glory or even a time of justice and prosperity. Jesus believed that God had asked him to be a human being *perfected by and for love in order to love*, so that, by his example, others could come to believe that what God had

---

11. Mark 14:62.
12. See, e.g., Job 25:6; Ps 8:4, 144:3, 146:3.
13. Isa 4:18.

CHAPTER 6   BELOVED OF GOD

manifested in Jesus might be manifested by and in anyone—anyone, that is, whose life conformed to Jesus' teachings.

We have now looked at Jesus as a unique personage in the history of Israel: as mystic, revolutionary, visionary, and beloved of God. He believed that God, as a loving father, had asked him to live out—that is, incarnate—the new relationship or covenant God was now seeking with his chosen people. That relationship was marked by love and incarnated by Jesus' choosing to sacrifice himself for the sake of his vision, his teachings about hope in human possibility and wholeness, and his insistence on mercy over judgment and forgiveness over pardon. Logically, this composite would have been woven together to form the basis for what later became Christianity. Christianity would have been focused on learning the "way" of Jesus in forming loving relationships, first with God and then with everyone else—particularly the marginalized. Christians would have been taught the way of surrender to love outlined in the Sermon on the Mount, and they would have learned what love looks like in practical terms from the example of Jesus himself. They would have understood baptism as a celebration of being anointed as God's very own son or daughter and would have met over a dinner table to remember and give thanks for the foretaste of the kingdom to come that Jesus had promised and exemplified in his own life and to share themselves with each other just as Jesus had done.

This is not what happened, however. Instead, the human Jesus was resurrected from the dead as a wholly spiritual Presence, confounding everyone who knew him and raising the issue once again, even more urgently, of what kind of Messiah he actually was. Indeed, so stunning were the events of the resurrection and its aftermath that finding an explanation for God's intent in the life—and now, death—of Jesus overshadowed every other consideration in the minds of those who knew him. Largely forgotten were Jesus' teachings on the kingdom of God. And, while it is possible to hear an echo of the vibrant hopefulness of Jesus' teaching in Christian liturgies today, his good news about the possibility of human transformation is mostly lost. In the following chapters, we will look at both how Jesus' core message was sidelined and how the image of a new kind of Messiah emerged from the empty tomb.

Chapter 7 Emergence of Christian Spirituality

WE HAVE NOTED PREVIOUSLY that God's revelation in the life of Jesus was unprecedented. But that uniqueness did not end with the death of the historical Jesus. There was a second part to God's revelation in Jesus—and it was not, as the church has long taught, that the post-resurrection events were a rubber stamp on the messianic expectations contained in the first part of the revelation. Rather, the second part of the revelation has its own distinct character and gravitas, describing multiple encounters with the risen Jesus both in the book of Acts of the Apostles (Acts) and in John's Gospel. These stories reflect a series of real and profound experiences of Jesus fully present and alive—to such an extent that the dying movement Jesus had inspired burst into life and began to convert people in record numbers.

Acts first takes up the story of Jesus after his death and resurrection, adding multiple new stories about post-resurrection encounters with the risen Jesus. These post-resurrection stories are not just about individual encounters; on the day of the Jewish feast of Pentecost, thousands of people from all over the diaspora witnessed a profound change in Jesus' disciples as they broke free of their fear of persecution and became evangelizers of the new gospel.[1] The power and joy of the disciples extended to every pilgrim who had journeyed to Jerusalem for the holiday, as each was enabled to hear the new gospel in their own language. The disciples soon began to baptize, heal, and cast out demons, both in their homeland and wherever they traveled to spread the gospel. The gifts of God's Spirit were so

---

1. Acts 2 *et seq.*

abundant that Paul had to admonish the members of the church in Corinth to strive for the gift of prophecy rather than merely enjoy the gift of speaking in tongues, since the former is edifying to the entire community while ". . . those who speak in a tongue do not speak to people but to God; for nobody understands them since they are speaking mysteries in the Spirit."[2] Acts concludes with the story of Paul's encounter with the risen Jesus on the Road to Damascus and Paul's and the disciples' experiences with the risen Jesus as they try to spread the good news beyond Israel.

In this chapter, we'll first look at whether such stories can be believed and then examine how Luke and John, the writers of Acts and the Gospel of John, respectively, understood their meaning and significance. The chapter concludes with a discussion of how the Gospel of John integrates the actual experience of divine encounter with the gospel of love that Jesus preached and lived.

The Post-Resurrection Stories

As a general matter, neither Luke nor John would have had difficulty believing in a divine encounter. In both early Christian and surrounding pagan cultures, it was more or less commonplace for humans to have run-ins with divine personages. Jesus was an historical human being, however, and not born immortal, so it became important to explain how, if Jesus had died, people were experiencing him as an immortal being. The obvious explanation was that Jesus had been raised from the dead *in his body,* just as Jewish tradition had promised to all righteous Jews at the end of time. And Jesus' resurrection, in turn, proved that he was the long-awaited Messiah, the one whose coming meant the time of the eschaton was fast approaching. The task as Luke and John saw it was three-fold: They had to establish, first, that it was indeed the rabbi Jesus whom everyone knew and loved that God had raised and, second, that Jesus was well and truly alive and could be experienced as alive. They also believed that they had to establish, once and for all, that Jesus was the Davidic Messiah. The story of Jesus' appearance before an assembled group of disciples illustrates the first point:

> They were startled and terrified, and thought they were seeing a ghost. [Jesus] said to them, "Why are you frightened, and why do doubts arise in your hearts? Look at my hands and my feet; for a ghost does not have flesh and bones as you see that I have." And

2. 1 Cor 14:2.

> when he said this, he showed them his hands and his feet. While in their joy they were disbelieving and still wondering, he said to them, "Have you anything here to eat?' They gave him a piece of broiled fish, and he took it in their presence."[3]

In the same vein, the writer of John's Gospel, also writing to gentiles, includes the story of "doubting Thomas," a disciple who was not present when Jesus first appeared to the disciples but whom the risen Jesus invited to actually place his hands inside the wounds of his crucifixion to prove that he was indeed Jesus.

To illustrate the point that Jesus was truly alive and could be experienced as alive, John's Gospel explains that Jesus might not appear as himself but might be disguised in other forms. Thus, Mary Magdalene mistakes the risen Jesus for a gardener, and Peter and John see a mysterious man cooking breakfast on the shore. In Luke's Gospel, the disciples on the Emmaus road see Jesus as a mysterious stranger. In such stories, Jesus is recognized when his followers experience a consoling sense of *shalom*, or they recognize his tender voice ("Jesus said to [Mary Magdalene], 'Mary'"[4]), or they recognize him as he breaks bread, or when an empty fishing net is suddenly teeming with fresh fish. The message is that, even if you didn't (or can't) actually see Jesus, you can experience his presence by his peace, his personal call, the rite he left his disciples, miracles, and—most of all—in the ancient messianic prophecies.

In other words, these early Christians, based on real spiritual experiences, deduced that Jesus must have been raised and, therefore, that Jesus must be the Messiah and, therefore, that the day of the Lord was imminent. We see how firmly held this sequence of belief was in Paul's first letter to the new church in Thessalonica. The members of the church were grieving because some of the community had died without having been raised from the dead. Paul reassured them that those who had already died would be the first to be resurrected on the Day of the Lord:

> But we do not want you to be uninformed, brothers and sisters, about those who have died, so that you may not grieve as others do who have no hope. For since we believe that Jesus died and rose again, even so, through Jesus, God will bring with him those who have died. For this we declare to you by the word of the Lord, that

---

3. Luke 24:37–42.
4. John 20:16.

we who are alive, who are left until the coming of the Lord, will by
no means precede those who have died.[5]

What we see, then, is that the post-resurrection stories became all about proving that Jesus had been resurrected and that he was, therefore, the Messiah, rather than *standing on their own as the advent of a new era of unmediated spiritual encounter*. To this day, seminarians take no courses in Christian spirituality but instead learn about the kind of systematic theology Paul introduced. Aside from such medieval classics as the *Cloud of Unknowing*, it was not until the 1960s, when Thomas Merton began to write about his experiences of the Divine, and the 1970s, when Father Thomas Keating and his associates began a systematic study of the Christian contemplative tradition, that anyone took Christian spirituality seriously. According to Fr Keating, he and his fellow monks got tired of seeing pilgrims pass their Benedictine monastery only to flock to the Buddhist ashram down the road!

John's Spirituality of Love

We have seen that the post-resurrection appearances once again raised the question of Jesus' identity and that Luke and John, in telling the stories, sought to establish, once and for all, that Jesus was the Davidic Messiah promised to Israel for the salvation of all people. John's Gospel as a whole, however, is unique among the gospels in that John was not concerned with establishing Jesus' messiahship by narrating the story of his life.

The best way to get a sense of just how different John's Gospel is from the earlier three is to start at the beginning of the gospel text:

> In the beginning was the Word, and the Word was with God, and the Word was God. He was in the beginning with God. All things came into being through him, and without him not one thing came into being. What has come into being in him was life, and the life was the light of all people. The light shines in the darkness, and the darkness did not overcome it . . . The true light, which enlightens everyone, was coming into the world.[6]

This is clearly metaphorical, not historical, language. Moreover, it doesn't hedge the issue of Jesus' identity but, from the start, proclaims what Jesus'

---

5. 1 Thess 4:13–15.
6. John 1:1–5, 9.

identity and mission were. Jesus is God's Word who, because the Word is a self-revelation of God, has existed for all eternity. This Word gives life to everything—the universe, the planets, human beings, and horseshoe crabs. Moreover, this life is so powerful that it can withstand all of the powers of darkness.

John's purpose was to demonstrate that, whether or not Jesus was the Davidic Messiah, it is possible for human beings to actually experience God's love just as Jesus (and Paul) did. Whereas the synoptic gospels respectively start with a genealogy of the Davidic Messiah (Matthew), Jesus' baptism (Mark), or a birth narrative (Luke), John's first story poses the provocative question, "What are you looking for?"[7] and his focus is to show how Jesus, as a result of his relationship with God, points the way to a humanity that can more closely experience and model the divine. John was not so much seeking to establish historical verisimilitude as he was trying to describe *the basis for faith* in Jesus as the Davidic Messiah. For John, what mattered was that we can experience the very beating heart of God's love in Jesus. In other words, while the synoptic gospels understand the good news to be that we can, like Jesus, become sons and daughters of God in this life by embracing Jesus' teachings and living as he did, John's Gospel offers us an exposition of what Christian mystical "spirituality" is all about—how God's spirit of love can be most truly and lavishly experienced. In this way, John's Gospel functions as the ultimate outcome of the process of transformation Jesus outlined in his Sermon on the Mount.

The gospel has four parts. After the mysterious prologue, the second part of the gospel is the "book of signs," consisting of seven miracles performed by Jesus, each of which reveals something about the nature of divine love. For example, when Jesus turns the water into fine wine at a wedding celebration, we are to understand that God's love flows freely as wine and is finer than anything we can imagine. When Jesus heals a man born blind, it is so that everyone may "see" that God's love heals lavishly and indiscriminately.[8] When Jesus converses with a Samaritan woman at an ancient well and then lets her know that he knows about her past illicit liaisons, it is to show that divine love knows no barriers of prejudice, ethnic or gender, and that God's love penetrates the deepest secrets of our hearts.[9] Interspersed among the signs are a variety of metaphors used by

7. John 1:38.
8. John 9.
9. See John 4:1–30.

CHAPTER 7   EMERGENCE OF CHRISTIAN SPIRITUALITY

Jesus to identify himself and his mission. These are the "I am" statements, echoing the response Yahweh gave to Moses when Moses asked Yahweh's identity. "I am the bread of life,"[10] "I am the way, the truth, and the life,"[11] and "I am the good shepherd"[12] are statements that not only align Jesus' mission with God's own but also proclaim Jesus as the only means by which God's love is truly manifested.

But it is the third part of John's Gospel, chapters 14 through 17, that captured my heart as a young woman. There we have Jesus at his most tender and most comforting. We can sense how much Jesus loved his disciples and how much they loved him: "Jesus knew that his hour had come to depart from this world and go to the Father. Having loved his own who were in the world, he loved them to the end."[13] In these chapters, Jesus casts the vision for his disciples, not by announcing the good news, nor by entrusting them with the rite of the last supper, but by commanding them to love each other:

> Little children, I am with you only a little longer. You will look for me; and as I said to the Jews so now I say to you, "Where I am going, you cannot come." I give you a new commandment, that you love one another. By this, everyone will know that you are my disciples, if you have love for one another.[14]

And, in order to demonstrate the nature of love, Jesus washed his disciples' feet, saying,

> ... [I]f I, your Lord and Teacher, have washed your feet, you also ought to wash one another's feet. For I have set you an example ... Very truly, I tell you, servants are not greater than their master, nor are messengers greater than the one who sent them.[15]

The heart of love as Jesus exemplified it is in humble service to the other.

But, equally, the experience of divine love is also about *receiving* that humble service of the beloved. This essential piece of the spirituality of love, so challenging to us as well as to Peter, entails acknowledging that we need and want the cleansing Jesus offers us. Jesus' own humility evokes ours and,

10. John 6:35.
11. John 14:6.
12. John 10:11.
13. John 13:1.
14. John 13:33–35.
15. John 13:14–16.

once the loving exchange has taken place, also evokes a desire to offer love back to God in the form of gratitude. Thus, we both see and experience the reality that the spirituality of love is a circle of offering, receiving, and offering back that is dynamic, self-sustaining, and eternal.[16]

Having cast this vision of the dynamics of divine love, Jesus next shows us how faith makes it possible. Faith, Jesus taught, means believing that, first of all, love originates in God and that Jesus' own life in service to others perfectly manifests that love: "If you know me, you will know my Father also. From now on, you do know him and have seen him."[17] Second, Jesus taught that faith also means believing that divine love can wholly interpenetrate and transform the human heart if we allow it:

> They who have my commandments [including the commandment to receive love offered] and keep them are those who love me; and those who love me will be loved by my Father, and I will love them and reveal myself to them . . . we will come to them and make our home with them.[18]

Jesus summed up these teachings in a lengthy prayer to God, beseeching God to unify the disciples and "those who will believe in me through their word"[19] in the knowledge that "[a]s you, Father, are in me and I am in you, may they also be in us, so that the world will believe that you sent me. The glory that you have given me I have given them, so that they may be one, as we are one."[20] Thus, it is ultimately the love God generously pours out to us, evoking our loving response, that binds us to each other and to God.

Over and over in the synoptic gospels, Jesus told those whom he had cured that it was their "faith" that made them "whole" or "has healed you."[21] But it is not until we reach John's gospel that we fully understand what Christian faith really consists of. Faith in what? Faith in who? we wonder. John's Gospel explains that our participation in the spirituality of love is instantiated by faith that God is the source of love, that God gives God's very self to us as love, and that we are co-participants in that love. This is why, at

---

16. To be noted here is the similarity of this understanding of divine love to descriptions of the Trinity, the belief that God is in three "persons"—Father, Son, and Holy Spirit–and that these three dimensions of God are in an eternal dance of self-giving love.

17. John 14:7.

18. John 14:21, 23.

19. John 17:20.

20. John 17:21–23.

21. Mark 5:31.

the end of the discourse on divine love, Jesus says, "I now call you friends ..."[22] Moreover, it implies that God finds us worthy to accept such a gift and trusts us to teach others that God's love can both be fully experienced in our lives as a union with God's very self and can be fully manifested in and through us to unite us with each other. Thus, *John's Gospel completes and provides the spiritual basis for Jesus' command to love* God above all things and to love our neighbors as we are loved.

The longing for unitive love finds expression in different ways in all religions—whether to become an enlightened Buddhist, or a Sufi ecstatic—but the point is that the Gospel of John is witness to the reality that *Christianity, at least as it was practiced by a small number of people around 100 CE, offered a spirituality of unitive love that was evidently seen as the whole point of God's intention through the person and ministry of Jesus*. While this understanding managed to resist banishment in some parts of the eastern church,[23] the idea that humans can enter into transforming union with the Divine was seen in the western church as spawning dangerous heresies.[24] The Church ended up by essentially sidelining John's core message—and, with it, the core identity and mission of both Jesus and Paul.

---

22. John 15:15.

23. The original "church" covered the entire extent of the Roman Empire, but it split in 1054 into the more "mystical" eastern orthodox traditions in the east and the more dogmatic Roman Catholic tradition in the west.

24. The most dangerous heresy in early Christianity was gnosticism. Gnosticism generally refers to a kind of secret knowledge of the redemptive power of Jesus that initiates to a particular sect might experience. This is not the same thing as mystical insight conferred on any person who goes in search of it. Gnosticism is exclusionary of other kinds of spiritual experience.

Chapter 8 A Risen Lord

THE MOST PERPLEXING QUESTION vexing Jesus' early followers post-resurrection was how to reconcile the Messiah they believed Jesus was with the prophecies of what he was supposed to be. In this chapter, we'll look at the struggle both Peter and Paul had with reconciling their avowed Judaism with the post-resurrection events they had personally witnessed. We'll look at where their analyses fall short and where their struggles eventually led them. This will allow us to speculate about how their sermons and writings formed the basis for the Messiah proclaimed by the evolving church.

Peter lived contemporaneously with Paul, but the similarities end there. While Acts records several eloquent sermons attributed to Peter, they cannot compare with the passionately reasoned theology Paul left as his legacy. Still, Peter's thought process became as much a part of Christian theology as Paul's writings, and the two in combination formed the theoretical basis for the church's first-, second-, and third-century debates about the nature of Jesus' messiahship.

Peter's Messiah

Peter's sermon at the Jewish feast of Pentecost, shortly after Jesus' resurrection, gives an almost visceral sense of how difficult it was for the disciples to make sense of Jesus' death and resurrection in terms of Jewish expectations. Peter was preaching to a huge crowd of fellow Jews gathered in Jerusalem for the celebration, and the entire crowd had just had an up-front visit from God's Spirit. Peter's task was to somehow convince his audience that Jesus was the predicted Messiah, even though he was clearly not the warrior-king described in the prophecies. Undaunted, Peter came up with four reasons why Jesus was the Davidic Messiah. First, Jesus had done many "deeds of power, wonders, and signs . . ."[1] Second, God had raised him from death.[2] Third, as a result, Jesus' flesh was not corrupted, consistent with God's promise to David that his descendant would not see the corruption of his flesh.[3] Fourth and last, Peter claimed that the Holy Spirit that he himself and the crowd had experienced could only be explained as having come from Jesus, now in an exalted state.[4]

All four of these arguments are very thin at best. As to the first argument—that Jesus could perform miracles—God had worked miracles throughout biblical history through those whom he chose, starting with Moses and the parting of the waters. Although this argument does not exclude Jesus, neither does it prove that he was the Davidic Messiah. Peter's second argument—that Jesus was the Davidic Messiah because God resurrected him from the dead—appears to conform to the facts; however, it, too, is faulty, because there is no suggestion in Hebrew scripture that God had promised to resurrect the Davidic Messiah. As to the third argument—that Psalm 16, believed to be written by King David, predicted that the Davidic Messiah would not experience corruption of the flesh—David is clearly offering a prayer *concerning himself*.[5] In the phrase, "I have said to the Lord, you are my Lord . . .," the Hebrew name "Adonai," meaning "Lord," was used to refer to God because it was unlawful to say or write God's holy name. So, David was praying to God as "Lord" and not to some future Messiah called

---

1. Acts 2:22.
2. Acts 2:24.
3. Acts 2:25–32, quoting Ps 16.
4. Acts 2:32–36, quoting Ps 110.
5. The pertinent part of Psalm 16 reads,

> Protect me, O God, for I take refuge in you;
> I have said to the Lord, "You are my Lord,
> my good above all other" . . .
> O Lord, you are my portion and my cup;
> it is you who uphold my lot . . .
> I have set the Lord always before me;
> because he is at my right hand I shall not fall.
> My heart, therefore, is glad and my spirit rejoices;
> my body also shall rest in hope.
> For you will not abandon me to the grave,
> nor let your holy one see the Pit . . . (Ps 16:1–10).

"Lord." Moreover, the Hebrew translation of the verse suggesting that a future "Lord" will not die reads, "For Thou wilt not abandon my soul to the nether-world; neither wilt thou suffer Thy godly one to see the pit."[6] Here, David is trusting that God would not abandon *David* to the "pit," another name for "Sheol," the place of darkness after death.

Moreover, none of Peter's arguments explain the utter ignominy of Jesus' death. *No* prophecy foretold that the warrior-king Davidic Messiah would die like a criminal in the hands of a conquering empire, since—in a culture in which one's death was the final statement about the holiness of one's life—any such prophecy would have been wholly inconsistent with messianic expectations. Not only was Jesus' death tragic but it would also have been viewed as a shameful reflection on his life and teachings. Nonetheless, Peter devised two novel arguments to explain this. First, tapping into the popular apocalyptic eschatology of the age, Peter taught that Jesus' victory over Israel's oppressors had just been *postponed* and not defeated. In fact, he argued, not only would Jesus return as the Messiah to usher in a new age of justice and prosperity for Israel, but also Jesus *had to die so that he could be resurrected as the first sign of the resurrection of all believers at that time.* This would have made sense to Peter's Jewish compatriots because Judaism had always looked forward to a time of general resurrection of the faithful, though in what form was always unclear. As a second novel argument, Peter expanded the characteristics previously associated with the Davidic Messiah to include prophecies of a "suffering servant." In an impassioned sermon given at the temple, after Peter had healed a man born lame, Peter explained that the healing had been accomplished by the "name" of Jesus and that Jesus' death was actually the ". . . way God fulfilled what he had foretold through all the prophets, that his Messiah would suffer."[7] Peter's prooftext was chapter 53 of the prophet Isaiah, quoted by Christians every Christmas: "Surely he has borne our infirmities and carried out our diseases; yet we accounted him stricken, struck down by God, and afflicted. But he was wounded for our transgressions, crushed for our iniquities; upon him was the punishment that made us whole, and by his bruises we are healed."[8]

It is obvious, however, that Isaiah was not referring—nor had any intention of referring—to any messiah figure, since there is nothing in the

---

6. Mechon Mamre, "Psalm 16:10."
7. Acts 3:17–19.
8. Isa 53:4–5.

prophecies about the Messiah suggesting that God would make the Messiah's suffering into the path of salvation for his people. That is, if Jesus was the "suffering servant" of Isaiah, he cannot, by definition, also be the Davidic Messiah, for the expectations associated with each are diametrically opposed to the other. Moreover, rabbinic interpretation of Isaiah's prophecy points out that chapter 53 is one of four servant songs, with the three previous plainly referring to Israel as God's servant.[9] Rabbinic tradition also interprets the change of narrator in this chapter to be the voices of all of the conquering kings of Israel who, when the messianic age comes, will both be humbled by Israel's steadfast faithfulness to the one true God and regret having caused Israel suffering over the millennia.[10]

Peter's struggle to fit Jesus into any plausible mold of a Davidic Messiah was finally eclipsed by a dream Peter had in which he saw a sheet being lowered from heaven holding all kinds of animals, reptiles, and birds. Peter heard a voice ordering him to kill and eat the animals, some of which were not kosher. Peter resisted, explaining that ". . . nothing profane or unclean has ever entered my mouth."[11] But the voice insisted, saying: "What God has made clean, you must not call profane."[12] The sheet was withdrawn into heaven; immediately thereafter, Peter was summoned to the home of a pious Roman centurion, Cornelius. Upon arriving at Cornelius' house, Peter saw that there was an assembly of gentiles—with whom he was forbidden to associate under Jewish purity laws. Cornelius related how he, too, had had a dream in which a heavenly figure told him that God had heard his prayers and that he should send for Peter to listen to what Peter had to say. At this, Peter exclaimed that he now understood that Jesus was "Lord *of all*," not only the people of Israel. "I now truly [understood] that God shows no partiality, but in every nation anyone who fears him and does what is right is acceptable to him."[13] This messiah was indeed a pious Jew; but, in his resurrection, he had become a new kind of prophesied Davidic

---

9. See, e.g., the book of Isaiah: "But you, Israel, my servant, Jacob, whom I have chosen, the offspring of Abraham, my friend . . ." (Isa 41:8–9); "But now hear, O Jacob, my servant, Israel whom I have chosen!" (Isa 44:1); "Remember these things, O Jacob, and Israel, for you are my servant; I formed you; you are my servant, O Israel . . ." (Isa 44:21).

10. See Isa 53:5 (recognizing their own "iniquity" as having caused the suffering); Isa 52:10 (regretting that they had "despised him and held him of no account").

11. Acts 10:14.

12. Acts 10:15.

13. Acts 10:35.

Messiah, not only for Jews who would accept a different kind of Messiah but also for everyone else. Jesus was "... anointed [by God] with the Holy Spirit and with power ... [He] went about doing good and healing all who were oppressed by the devil, for God was with him ... We are witnesses to all that he did both in Judea and in Jerusalem ... and [we] ate and drank with him after he rose from the dead."[14]

Most radically, Peter came to believe that God's blessing was not limited to those who lived under and obeyed the ritual laws but rather was available to anyone with a pious and righteous heart who was willing to believe in what Peter and the other disciples had personally witnessed. Of course, the primacy of purity of heart over right observance had been the very centerpiece of Jesus' own teaching; however, until Peter's epiphany, all Jews believed that the coming of the Davidic Messiah and obedience to the laws of Moses were inseparable and that the coming of the Messiah would be the final vindication of the righteousness of the laws and of the role Israel was to play as a "light to the nations." Peter's new revelation was that it was now possible to continue to claim that Jesus was the Messiah prophesied of old because he had "come from the Jews"—not because he resembled the prophecies about the Davidic Messiah in any way. This new kind of Davidic Messiah was not bound by the laws of the ancestors nor was he a vindication of the law or of God's special destiny for Israel. Instead, God's blessing and invitation to holiness were available to anyone who sought the particular way of salvation taught and lived by Jesus.[15]

The evolution in Peter's understanding of God's revelation in the life and teachings of Jesus, in light of the resurrection, is astonishing. He started out trying to prove that Jesus was *the* Davidic Messiah but, perhaps because even he knew that there was no precedent for that in scripture, he began to preach that Jesus was *a* Davidic Messiah—just not the warrior-king type of Messiah. This "suffering servant" Davidic Messiah was Israel's gift to Jews and gentiles alike, and the availability of his saving power lay not in observance of Jewish law but in proclaiming this new Messiah as Lord. Yet, Peter remained convinced until his death that, even though the Davidic Messiah had come in a new form, it was nonetheless as much part and parcel of the ancient prophecies as the earlier warrior-king predictions.

---

14. Acts 10:38–40.
15. Acts 10:37 *et seq.*

CHAPTER 8   A RISEN LORD

Paul's Messiah

St. Paul, formerly Saul of Tarsus, is one of those saints you'd love to hate. He was dogmatic, irascible, and doctrinaire. But he was also brilliant, fiercely loyal to his cause, and convinced that God had uniquely singled him out to spread the gospel to the Roman world. Paul's writings, in the form of the letters he wrote to the various churches he founded, are the earliest writings in the Christian canon and, unlike the gospels, these writings are wholly original to Paul and not cobbled together from other sources.[16] Even those with no desire to explore Christianity have heard these lines from St. Paul's first letter (of two) to the new Christian community in Corinth, Greece:

> If I speak in the tongues of mortals and of angels, but do not have love, I am a noisy gong or a clanging cymbal. And if I have prophetic powers, and understand all mysteries and all knowledge, and I have all faith, so as to remove mountains, but do not have love, I am nothing . . . Love is patient; love is kind; love is not envious or boastful or arrogant or rude . . . It does not rejoice in wrongdoing, but rejoices in the truth. It bears all things, believes all things, hopes all things, endures all things. Love never ends . . .[17]

This is perhaps the most gorgeous paean to love ever written. It would have touched Jesus to his core.

Paul was a devout and zealous Pharisee whose mission was to stop the Jesus movement in its tracks and see Jesus' followers stoned for blasphemy. Paul was on his way to Damascus with letters to the synagogues from the High Priest to warn them about "any who belonged to the Way"[18] when suddenly a light from heaven flashed around him. He fell to the ground and heard a voice saying to him, "Saul, Saul, why do you persecute me?" He asked, "Who are you, Lord?" The reply came, "'I am Jesus, whom you are persecuting. But get up and enter the city, and you will be told what you are to do' . . . Saul got up from the ground, and though his eyes were open, he

---

16. To be noted, however, is that not all of Paul's letters are thought to be authored by him. It was common practice in ancient times for others to write "in the name of" another. Of the thirteen epistles attributed to Paul, only Galatians, Romans, 1 Thessalonians, Philippians, 1 Corinthians, 2 Corinthians, and Philemon were likely penned by Paul. They others are viewed as faithfully consistent with what Paul actually taught. An analogy might be the difference between a Bellini painted by the original artist and a painting by his student or a member of the School of Bellini.

17. 1 Cor 13:1–8.

18. Acts 9:2.

could see nothing . . . For three days, he was without sight and neither ate nor drank."[19] After Paul was baptized, he retreated to the deserts of Arabia, where he remained for three years before finally journeying to Jerusalem to meet the apostles Peter, James, and John in person.[20]

Paul lived contemporaneously both with Jesus and with the fledgling community of Jesus' disciples and, although Paul never met Jesus personally, his encounter with the risen Jesus caused a wrenching identity crisis that eventually led to his joining the new Jesus sect and becoming its most ardent evangelist.[21] Paul's encounter with the risen Jesus changed Paul's entire understanding of the nature of salvation, and the theology Paul created bearing witness to that became the basis for Christian theology as we know it. Moreover, because Paul maintained a close working relationship with both Peter and James, as well as many other members of the Jesus community, we can assume that Paul's new theology could not have departed in any significant way from what the disciples had learned directly from the Master himself. On the other hand, Jesus was a storyteller, not a theologian, and, while Jesus had had his own personal revelation of God, he was in no position to reflect on God's purpose in the events after his death!

Paul's thought process, like Peter's, was by no means static but evolved as he traveled and taught—and met with consistent rejection by his fellow Jews. But, while Peter struggled to fit the "suffering servant" model into Jewish messianic promises, the starting point for Paul's theology of messiahship was his personal encounter with the risen Jesus on the road to Damascus. This experience convinced Paul that God was doing something entirely new. Paul called this new messianic phenomenon "Christ Jesus."

At the most superficial level, *christos* is simply the Greek equivalent for "anointed one" or "messiah." For Paul and the early church, though, "Christ" was the resurrected Jesus, a living persona who could appear in any number of forms—as he did, for example, on the road to Emmaus or to Paul on the road to Damascus. This mystical Christ had once been the historical Jesus, a holy Jewish rabbi, whom God had transformed into a living spiritual presence:

---

19. Acts 9:3–9.
20. See Gal 1.
21. By that time, the members of the new Jesus sect were living both in and around Jerusalem with James, Jesus' brother as their leader, as well as in Antioch (Syria) under Peter's leadership.

> So it is with resurrection of the dead. What is sown is perishable, what is raised is imperishable. If it is sown in dishonor, it is raised in glory. It is sown in weakness, it is raised in power. It is sown a physical body, it is raised a spiritual body. Thus it is written, "The first man, Adam, became a living being," the last Adam became a life-giving spirit . . .[22]

Paul described this persona as "Jesus Christ" or "Christ Jesus"—that is, both an historical person and now (and forever) a wholly spiritual being. This Jesus Christ was the Messiah, the one whom God ". . . promised beforehand through his prophets in holy scriptures, the gospel concerning his Son, who was descended from David according to the flesh and was declared to be Son of God with power according to the spirit of holiness by resurrection from the dead, Jesus Christ our Lord, through whom we have received grace . . ."[23] The historical Jesus, who believed that he was God's "son" because he was chosen by God to embody God's love and thus serve as the agent of God's plan for Israel had, according to Paul, been "declared to be Son of God . . . by resurrection from the dead."[24]

Over time, Paul's theology about the nature of Christ became even more radical. In his letter to the Philippians, Paul quoted the lyrics of what seems to be a hymn of the early church, in which Jesus Christ was said to be "equal with God." This Son of God ". . . though he was in the form of God, did not regard equality with God . . . but emptied himself, taking the form of a slave, being born in human likeness . . ."[25] Finally and most radically, this wholly spiritual "man" did not first come into being at the resurrection but had been dwelling with God in heaven all along: "The first man was from the earth . . . the second man is from heaven."[26]

It is difficult to reconcile this theology with Judaism's strict monotheism, which Paul would never have disavowed. But we can gain some insight into how Paul reconciled his monotheism with his views on the nature of Jesus Christ by looking at Paul's direct rebuke to new Corinthian converts who were still offering food to idols and then eating it (a universal pagan practice). To these Corinthians, Paul exclaimed,

---

22. 1 Cor 15:42–46.
23. Rom 1:2–6.
24. Rom 1:4.
25. Phil 2:5–7.
26. 1 Cor 15:47.

> ... [A]s to the eating of food offered to idols, we know that "no idol in the world really exists," and that "there is no God but one" (the Jewish *shema*). Indeed, even though there may be so-called gods in heaven or earth—as in fact there are many gods and many lords—yet for us there is one God, the Father, from whom are all things and for whom we exist, and one Lord, Jesus Christ, through whom are all things and through whom we exist.[27]

While acknowledging that there may be many gods and many lords, Paul told the new believers that, *for us*, there is only one God—the God of Israel, Yahweh/*Theos*, and one Messiah/*Christos*/*Adonai*/*Kyrios*/Lord. To affirm that Jesus is Lord is to acknowledge that the one and indivisible God has empowered Jesus Christ to be God's messianic agent and, as such, the Lord or master of all. It thus stops short of claiming that the Messiah shares the same divine nature as Yahweh/*Theos*.

As God's messianic agent, Jesus Christ would return to complete the messianic promises of old. But Paul's version of how this would occur is markedly different from Peter's or from Judaism in general. Jews then as now believed that the coming of the Messiah and the messianic kingdom of justice and prosperity would occur after the Son of Man arrived and presided over a time of catastrophe and cosmic disturbance. The coming of the Messiah would be the capstone of the apocalypse, and the Messiah's role would be the Lord of the eternal eschaton promised to righteous Jews. But, for Paul, it would be the Messiah—and not the Son of Man—who would be the agent of the apocalypse. Christ would return, claiming all who belong to him and, at the same time, crush "every ruler and every authority and power."[28] The last power to be destroyed would be death; from thence forward, anyone who confessed Jesus as Lord and Messiah would experience resurrection from the dead. Then, once everything was "subjected under his [Christ's] feet," the eschaton would come, and Christ would hand over his kingdom to God.[29] Thus, for both Peter and Paul, the apocalypse started with the resurrection, Jesus being the "first fruits" of those who would follow later. To this belief, Paul added the belief that Christ's second coming (or *parousia*) would initiate the beginning of the end, followed by the vanquishing of all of Israel's enemies and the advent

---

27. 1 Cor 8:4–6.
28. 1 Cor 8:25.
29. 1 Cor 15:26–28.

of a new age. At that point, Christ would take his place alongside God in the heavenly realms.

Weaving the strands of Peter's and Paul's thinking about the messiahship of Jesus together produces a composite Christian version in which Jesus fulfills the Jewish prophecies by being the suffering servant described by Isaiah, while also, because of his resurrection, becoming Jesus Christ, a spiritual presence who is equal to God. Belief in God's action in Christ Jesus was sufficient for salvation, independent of Jewish observance. Moreover, this new Messiah was not inconsistent with the Jewish expectations of a Messiah warrior-king because the new Messiah, Jesus Christ, would return and display all of the characteristics associated with the ancient prophecies. His fulfillment as Israel's Messiah warrior-king had only been delayed.

The most eloquent statement of these beliefs can be found in Paul's stirring testimony before the Herodian King Agrippa when called up on charges of blasphemy. Now at the end of his ministry, Paul stated without equivocation that Jesus was the culmination of the promises made to Israel. Reminding Agrippa that he, Paul, was a Pharisee and thus an expert in Jewish law, he argued that there can be no doubt that Yahweh has the power to raise the dead. Paul argued that he had preached exactly what Moses and the prophets said would happen: The Christ must suffer and, being the first to rise from the dead, would proclaim salvation both to Israel and to the gentiles. As support for this preaching, Paul told of his vision of the risen Jesus on the road to Damascus and his conviction, based on the prophets of old, that Yahweh was now calling both Jews and gentiles to repent and begin to act in ways that showed their repentance.[30]

---

30. See Acts 26.

Chapter 9 Paul's Witness

THAT PAUL SO CLEARLY understood the generosity and dynamism of divine love and Jesus' perfect witness to it should have served as the capstone of Paul's legacy. But, as we have already seen, Paul's theology was greatly influenced by some of the most powerful assumptions in Judaism, as well as by his struggle to make sense of Jesus' shameful death. These factors, together with his own profound conversion experience, thrust Paul into the lifelong internal conflict we see mirrored in his letters. What kind of Messiah was Jesus if he was clearly not the prophesied warrior-king? If Paul had been "saved" by a spiritual encounter with Jesus, what good, then, did Torah serve?

Moreover, Paul's thinking did not remain static during his lifetime but evolved along with his own sense of mission. To the early—largely Jewish—audience, Paul preached a simple message of a second coming of the Messiah, the imminent arrival of the end times, and the resurrection of righteous believers. Over time, though, as Paul came to believe that his primary mission was to preach the good news as he saw it to a pagan audience, Paul was compelled to fashion a theology that addressed the difference between polytheism and its associated observances and the monotheistic God of Israel. This thrust Paul into the most agonizing theological struggle he faced: how to explain to potential Jewish and pagan converts alike that the God of Israel's plan for salvation was now radically different than the Hebrew scriptures predicted, and the means of salvation—that is, obedience to the law of Moses—was now optional for pagan converts.

In this chapter, we'll consider the aspects of Paul's theology that are identical to Jesus' teachings. Then, we'll identify what was new in Paul's teachings and what might—or might not—have been acceptable to Jesus or to Paul's fellow Jews. Finally, we'll speculate about the impact of Paul's theology on the evolution of Christianity.

The Big Picture

The broad strokes of Paul's theology as it emerged from the tensions mentioned above were entirely consistent with Jesus' teachings. In particular, there are three elements that form the core of both of their belief systems: the primacy of love and forgiveness, God' desire for conversion of the human heart, and the imminent arrival of the end times.

The Primacy of Love and Forgiveness

Love featured foremost in both Paul's and Jesus' teachings. Paul had experienced that love in a deeply personal way directly from the risen Jesus, who—instead of judging and punishing Paul for his persecution of the new quasi-Jewish sect—showed only mercy and forgiveness. And, in perhaps the most telling aspect of deep love, Jesus saw in Paul what Paul could not see in himself: a new identity and a new vocation. Thus, we hear Paul repeating, nearly verbatim, these portions of the Sermon on the Mount: "Bless those who persecute you; bless and do not curse them . . . Live in harmony with one another; do not be haughty, but associate with the lowly . . . Do not repay evil for evil . . . No, if your enemies are hungry, feed them; if they are thirsty, give them something to drink . . . Do not be overcome by evil, but overcome evil with good."[1] Whatever else Paul might have believed, he clearly understood the depth and the demands of the kind of love Jesus taught and gave witness to.

The Possibility of Human Transformation

One of the most moving passages in Paul's letter to the Christian community in Rome is found in chapter 14. There, Paul chastises members of the community for judging other members' beliefs and rituals around food. "I know and am persuaded in the Lord Jesus that nothing is unclean in itself;

---

1. Rom 12:14, 16, 20–21.

but it is unclean for anyone who thinks it unclean."[2] For Paul, as for Jesus, sin does not lie in failing to perform specified rituals but resides more deeply in a heart that judges others who hold different views. "Some judge one day to be better than another, while others judge all days to be alike," Paul points out.[3] Different people hold differing views, but this reality is overshadowed by the deeper invitation to live in gratitude for whatever God provides and in the belief that God is alive in the risen Christ, who is eternally extending the invitation *to all* to accept God's lavish, unconditional love. "We do not live to ourselves, and we do not die to ourselves. If we live, we live to the Lord, and if we die, we die to the Lord; so then whether we live to whether we die, we are the Lord's."[4] For Paul, as for Jesus, it is faith in the powerful love of God that changes human hearts and reduces the various disagreements about praxis to secondary importance.

Yet, the issue of the role of praxis over faith in God's salvation plan haunted Paul throughout his life as a missionary. Because the new religion appealed to pagans more than to Jews, Paul had to struggle with the question of whether observance of the laws of Israel now played *any* role in salvation. He finally came to believe that God was now extending the promises made to Israel to anyone who confessed the risen Christ. Paul's letter to the fledgling Christian community in Rome shows him at his polemical best, trying to reconcile his former faith system with the newfound revelation of the risen Christ. Paul's accommodation was to find no fault in a pious Jew who obeys the sacred law nor to judge gentiles for not obeying the law—so long as their actions conform to the law's basic premises:

> For it is not the hearers of the law who are righteous in God's sight, but the doers of the law who will be justified. When gentiles, who do not possess the law, do instinctively what the law requires, these, though they do not have the law, are a law to themselves. They show that what the law requires is written on their hearts . . .[5]

Paul reasoned that, since Jews and gentiles are equally susceptible in their failure to live out what they know to be right, God's judgment and God's salvation will fall equally on both:

---

2. Rom 14:13.
3. Rom 14:5.
4. Rom 14:7.
5. Rom 2:13–16.

CHAPTER 9   PAUL'S WITNESS

> For he will repay according to each one's deeds: to those who by patiently doing good seek for glory and honor and immortality, he will give eternal life; while for those who are self-seeking and who obey not the truth but wickedness, there will be wrath and fury. There will be anguish and distress for everyone who does evil, the Jew first and also the Greek, but glory and honor and peace for everyone who does good, the Jew first and also the Greek. For God shows no partiality.[6]

The Imminence of the End Times

Both Jesus and Paul lived in a time of widespread belief that the end times were near. For the more radical Jews, such as the monastic Essene community and John the Baptist, it would come in the form of warfare between "the sons of darkness" and the "sons of light." The "sons of darkness" were the established Jewish elite that Jesus so often challenged, while the "sons of light" were the Essenes. For less ascetic Jews, which included Jesus, the eschaton would take the form prophesied by the writer of the book of Daniel: The world would devolve into constant warfare, famine, earthquakes, and lawlessness.[7] At a cosmic level, stars would fall from the sky, and the sun would be darkened. All of this would portend the coming of the "Son of Man," who would gather the righteous survivors (the "elect") from the ends of the earth into heaven.[8] In order to be prepared for this impending catastrophe, Jesus counseled his followers to remain "awake" because no one—not even he—knew when the time would come.[9]

Areas of Inconsistency

As much as the broad strokes of Paul's theology were consistent with what Jesus taught (and believed), there are areas of inconsistency within each area of general agreement. The primacy of love and forgiveness was, for Jesus, at the heart of all of his actions—his teaching, his healing, and his dying. That love resulted from his direct experience of the unconditional love of God. For Paul, however, there is an implicit condition that we can know

6. Rom 2:4–11.
7. Dan 7.
8. See Mark 13:19–27; Matt 24.
9. See Matt 25:13.

God's unconditional love *so long as* we also believe in Jesus as God's Christ. In interposing belief in Christ between us and God, Paul sets a condition on the otherwise unconditional love of God, thereby establishing the hallmark of what would become Christianity.

With respect to the possibility of the transformation of the human heart, Paul and Jesus differed in the value of praxis in spiritual maturation. For Paul, differences in religious practices matter only insofar as they encourage charitable action. If charitable action occurs independently of any particular praxis, the issue becomes moot. Jesus, on the other hand, taught spiritual transformation through praxis, with praxis being the essential prerequisite to the opening of the human heart to receive God's love. Religious men and women from the earliest times bear witness to the power of Jesus' "way" to transform lives.

Paul's Evolving Theology

Paul's theology was by no means static, however; it evolved as he traveled and taught—and as he met with consistent rejection by his fellow Jews. Here, we'll take a look at some of Paul's most obvious extrapolations from what Jesus taught, particularly his theory of the *parousia* or second coming, his extrapolation of the kingdom of God as synonymous with the *parousia*, and his definition of the good news as atonement for sin.

The Apocalypse as the second coming

Jews, then as now, believed that the coming of the Messiah and the messianic kingdom will occur after the Son of Man presides over a time of catastrophe and cosmic turbulence. Paul, however, had an alternative understanding of just how the events of the last days would unfold. It would be Jesus, a triumphant warrior Messiah, who would return, and not the mysterious Son of Man:

> For since we believe that Jesus died and rose again, even so, through Jesus, God will bring with him those who have died. For this we declare to you by the word of the Lord, that we who are alive, who are left until the coming of the Lord, will by no means precede those who have died. For the Lord himself, with a cry of command, with the archangel's call and with the sound of God's

trumpet, will descend from heaven, and the dead in Christ will rise first . . .[10]

Everything Paul taught about the saving acts of God in Christ was determined by his belief in a fairly immediate second coming.

But Paul's polemic did not end there, for he also taught that waiting with the faith that Jesus would soon return *had saving power in itself*:

> But you are not in the flesh; you are in the Spirit, since the Spirit of God dwells in you. Anyone who does not have the Spirit of Christ does not belong to him. But if Christ is in you, though the body is dead because of sin, the Spirit is life because of righteousness. If the Spirit of him who raised Jesus from the dead dwells in you, he who raised Christ from the dead will give life to your mortal bodies also through his Spirit that dwells in you.[11]

In other words, the power of faith that God has given us is his very Spirit. This same Spirit raised Jesus into eternal life as the Christ and it has the power to change the very identity of the believers in the *here and now*: ". . . [F]or all who are led by the Spirit of God are children of God. For you did not receive a spirit of slavery to fall back into fear, but you have received a spirit of adoption. When we cry, 'Abba, Father!' it is the very Spirit bearing witness with our spirit that we are children of God, and if children, then heirs, heirs of God and joint heirs with Christ . . ."[12] If we believe that God's Spirit indwells, we can actually claim the same relationship with God that Jesus did.

The Coming of the Kingdom of God as the Second Coming

Stunningly, Paul barely mentioned what was, for Jesus, the reason he accepted his vocation and his death. When Paul did mention the kingdom of God, it is clear that the kingdom was not a potentiality in the here and now but rather a spiritual state in full communion "with Christ" in the "heavenly places":

> But God, who is rich in mercy, out of the great love with which he loved us even when we were dead through our trespasses, made us alive together with Christ—by grace you have been saved—and

10. 1 Thess 4:14–16.
11. Rom 8:9–11.
12. Rom 8:14–17.

raised us up with him and seated us with him in the heavenly places in Christ Jesus . . .[13]

The kingdom of God was the promise of the future bliss of ". . . righteousness and peace and joy in the Holy Spirit."[14]

It would be a mistake, though, to think that Paul believed that the "heavenly places" were an actual locale. For Paul, and for all Jews, heaven was the sole domain of God's throne and God's angelic courtiers. Neither Jews nor newly converted Christians were to hope to go to heaven after death. Rather, what Paul intended to convey was that anyone who was "in Christ" was as fully spiritually alive as Christ during their mortal lives and thus already in a state of "heaven." It was because of this belief that Paul repeatedly exhorted new believers to concentrate on godly living:

> [D]o not gratify the desires of the flesh. For what the flesh desires is opposed to the Spirit, and what the Spirit desires is opposed to the flesh . . . Now the works of the flesh are obvious: fornication, impurity, licentiousness, idolatry sorcery, enmities, strife, jealousy, anger, quarrels, dissensions, factions, envy, drunkenness, carousing, and things like these. I am warning you, as I warned you before: those who do such things will not inherit the kingdom of God.[15]

Throughout, Paul was especially adamant about the sin of fornication. Strictly speaking, fornication meant having sexual relations between two unmarried people. This would include consensual sex and prostitution. But Paul, as a Pharisee, would also have meant "idolatrous fornication," the term historically referring to idolatry in general, as well as unrighteous behavior or worship of anything other than God.[16] Moreover, the term "fornication" would have resonated in Paul with passages such as Ezekiel 16, in which the prophet describes how God took Jerusalem as God's bride, cleansing and anointing her, and adorning her with gorgeous garments and jewelry, so that Israel's idolatry would have been a rupture of this marital relationship.

Yet, Paul's adamancy seems exaggerated even by these standards. This is likely due to the fact that, as a Pharisee, Paul believed in the literal

---

13. Eph 2:4–6.
14. Rom 14:17.
15. See Gal 5:17–21.
16. See Col 3:1–11.

resurrection of the physical body that would be reunited with the spirit after death. Indeed, Paul's worldview was that the resurrection of Jesus as the Christ was the kick-off, so to speak, of restoration of the world as God had originally designed it. So it would have been essential for the newly converted not only to "cleanse the thoughts of their hearts"[17] but also to prepare the body for eternal life.

> The body is not meant for fornication but for the Lord, and the Lord for the body. And God raised the Lord and will also raise us by his power. Do you not know that your bodies are members of Christ? Should I therefore take the members of Christ and make them members of a prostitute? Never! Do you not know that whoever is united to a prostitute becomes one body with her?[18]

Salvation through Justice

For Jesus, the good news of salvation was that a merciful and loving God was now showing his people, through Jesus' example, that the time had finally arrived for Israel to embody her destiny as a kingdom of priests. It would be Israel's converted heart that would serve as the change agent for a different world order. For Paul, the good news was that Jesus' willing sacrifice of himself was the ultimate solution to the problem of human sin. Believing this to be the truth, together with leading a godly life worthy of such a sacrifice, is what would assure the believer of a place in God's heavenly kingdom at the second coming.

This theology of sacrificial atonement was natural to Paul because, as discussed earlier, Second Temple Judaism held that God's justice required some sort of sacrificial offering in order to restore the sinner to God's favor. We have previously noted that these sacrifices took the form of various "first-fruit" offerings, made to honor God's bounty and faithfulness, and various "sin" offerings," made to restore the relationship between the sinner and God that sin had ruptured. Paul, however, took this system in a different direction, as he wrestled with the larger question of whether the law (including those regulating temple sacrifice) had been eclipsed by the death and resurrection of Jesus as Christ.

---

17. Anonymous, *The Cloud of Unknowing*.
18. 1 Cor 6:13–16. See Wright, *Paul for Everyone*, 205.

Paul came up with at least three theories to explain the cross—the first based on Jesus' righteousness and the second two embracing two different atonement theories. Whichever theory satisfactorily explained why Jesus had to die and why God had resurrected him, Paul was convinced that salvation was first and foremost about God's grace, the source of boundless mercy and forgiveness. It was grace that was unleashed by Jesus' sacrifice on the cross; moreover, it was grace that makes observance of the law unnecessary:

> ... [Y]ou have died to the law through the body of Christ, so that you may belong to another, to him who has been raised from the dead ... so that we are slaves not under the old written code but in the new life of the Spirit ... for sin will have no dominion over you, since you are not under law but under grace.[19, 20]

As to exactly what caused the release of this grace, Paul theorized that it was Jesus' consent to be God's Passover sacrificial lamb. Recalling the exodus from Egypt, the most seminal event in Israel's history, in which God decided to kill all of the Egyptian firstborn children, God warned the Israelites to put the blood of a newly slaughtered lamb on their doorposts so that God would know to "pass over" them. In the same way, Paul reasoned, Jesus' death was innocent blood spilled so that God would "pass over" our sin:

> But now, apart from the law, the righteousness of God has been disclosed ... for all who believe ... since all have sinned and fall short of the glory of God; they are now justified by his grace as a gift, through the redemption that is in Christ Jesus, whom God put forward as a sacrifice of atonement by his blood, effective through faith. He did this to show his righteousness, because in his divine forbearance he had passed over the sins previously committed ...[21]

Jesus' willing surrender to and trust in God revealed his own righteousness and simultaneously demonstrated the unrighteousness of the law that would put an innocent person to death. In the face of injustice, violence, and retribution, Jesus presents the face of faith and forgiveness.

Moreover, this righteousness can never die and, according to Paul, now intercedes between our sin and God's justice: "... [I]f Christ is in

---

19. Rom 7:4.
20. Rom 6:14.
21. Rom 3:25.

you, though the body is dead because of sin, the Spirit is life because of righteousness . . . Who is to condemn? It is Christ Jesus, who died, yes, who was raised, who is at the right hand of God, who indeed intercedes for us . . ."[22] Thus, we need never again fear that our sin will separate us from God's love: "Who will separate us from the love of Christ? Will hardship, or distress, or persecution . . .? No, in all these things we are more than conquerors through him who loved us."[23] Our sin is forever more than compensated for by Jesus' righteousness.

Nonetheless, as suggested, Paul did not seem satisfied with the paschal lamb theory of the cross, because he also argued two additional theories, both based on God's overriding need for justice. The first is a "ransom" theory: that God will spare humanity from judgment if God is presented with a suitable enough ransom. Quoting what is apparently an early church hymn, Paul advises his disciple, Timothy, that God ". . . desires everyone to be saved and to come to the knowledge of the truth. For 'there is one God; there is also one mediator between God and humankind, Christ Jesus, himself human, who gave himself a ransom for all.'"[24] Thus, Jesus spares us from the justice of God, heals a relationship broken by sin, and restores the original "at-one-ment" between humans and God.

The second atonement theory is known as the "substitutionary/vicarious atonement" theory. Here, Paul theorized that Jesus was more like the scapegoat described in the book of Leviticus,[25] in which God required the Israelites to find a spotless goat, heap the goat with all of their sins, and send it away into the wilderness. In the same vein, God offered up an innocent person to stand in for all of humanity, taking humanity's sin on himself. "What then are we to say about these things? If God is for us, who is against us? He who did not withhold his own Son, but gave him up for all of us, will he not with him also give us everything else?"[26] This theory took hold in the earliest days of the church as the "suffering servant" theory discussed earlier.

22. Rom 8:34–35.
23. Rom 8:35–39.
24. 1 Tim 2:5–6.
25. The origin of this theory can be found in the book of Leviticus, in which the Israelites were commanded to send a spotless goat into the wilderness to carry all of the sins and impurities of the people away from the community—never to return (Lev 16:10).
26. Rom 8:31–33.

How can we explain why Paul argued different theories of the cross? As noted earlier, the requirement of atonement for sin was normative for any Jew and written into the Hebrew scriptures. On the other hand, for Paul, as for any Jew, the idea that God would sacrifice his own son contravened Israel's longstanding abhorrence of human/child sacrifice. Paul's way of getting around this problem was to theorize that God had not sacrificed his son but had rather sacrificed God's own Self, in the form of Christ.[27] Moreover, according to this rationale, this sacrifice was so perfect that it would serve as the definitive atonement for all human sin, once and for all:

> For while we were still weak, at the right time, Christ died for the ungodly ... God proves his love for us in that while we still were sinners Christ died for us. Much more surely then, now that we have been justified by his blood, will we be saved through him from the wrath of God.[28]

Both the righteousness and the atonement theories of the cross fully explain the salvific nature of Jesus' death, and belief in any of the three would be enough to ensure that the new believer would join Jesus at the second coming.

It is thus nothing short of tragic that, for centuries, the church has taught that the *good news* is that God sacrificed his son in order to free us from our sinfulness. This is *bad news* on so many levels that, rather than reveal biblical truth, it demonstrates the unquestioned power of the church over centuries to convince its flock of baseless theology. On the first level, there is no textual authority for the idea that Jesus willingly went to his execution believing, somehow, that he was saving humankind by his sacrifice. Moreover, the seminal story of Abraham's near sacrifice of his son found in the book of Genesis directly confronts and confounds the idea of human sacrifice.[29]

On the next level, even assuming Yahweh decided to do something wholly contrary to his character by sacrificing a human being, Jewish

---

27. Phil 2:6–11.
28. Rom 5:6.
29. It will be recalled that God ordered Abraham to offer his son, Isaac, as a sacrifice, to test Abraham's faith in God. Abraham was at the point of raising the knife when God intervened, supplying a ram instead. This story not only shows that God does not demand or need human sacrifice, but it forms the very foundation of one of the deepest of all of the beliefs about Yahweh within Jewish scripture and wisdom literature—the theme of "testing and reprieve." God tests Israel to the limit of Israel's endurance, but then always shows mercy and provides for Israel's needs.

scripture consistently distinguishes Yahweh from the surrounding pagan gods to whom human sacrifice was made by portraying Yahweh as showing mercy rather than insisting on ritual atonement—of any kind.[30] We find a direct analogy to God's purported sacrifice of Jesus early in Israel's history when, during the long journey to the promised land, the people of Israel lost faith in Yahweh's promises and fashioned a golden calf to worship in His stead. This so angered Yahweh that he threatened their annihilation. Moses interceded, pleading for forgiveness on behalf of the people, and offering his own death as a substitute for their slaughter. Yahweh relented, manifesting his glory in passionate mercy and long-suffering love rather than in retributive atonement.[31] To emphasize: *It was Moses' self-abnegating love for the people, not his physical sacrifice, that evoked God's forgiveness and mercy.* Moses' righteousness alone served to atone for Israel's apostasy.

Later on, it became the role of the priests to serve as intercessors for Israel's sin through the offering of *kofer*, or a propitiatory gift, in the form of the fruits of the land or household animals.[32] These priestly practices continued throughout Jewish history as the *only appropriate way of atonement* for serious offenses against God's righteousness and justice until the destruction of the temple for a final time in 70 CE. At that time, Judaism abandoned sacrificial practices altogether, opting instead for the heartfelt repentance that had been stressed by the prophets Amos, Hosea, Micah, and Isaiah. These prophets taught that, while a righteous God requires justice, he is not looking for payback but rather restoration of broken relationships, asking only that we acknowledge our sin, ask the forgiveness of both God and those whom we have hurt, and vow not to sin again:

> Against you only have I sinned . . . And so you are justified when you speak and upright in your judgment . . . Had you desired it, I would have offered sacrifice, but you take no delight in burnt-offerings. The sacrifice of God is a troubled spirit; a broken and contrite heart, O God, you will not despise.[33]

---

30. Blood sacrifice of an innocent animal was required only for grave sins. Blood was understood to be the life force, or soul, of every living thing and so, for grave sins, it was appropriate that the life of the soul of the one (the sacrificial animal) was given in order to restore the soul of the other (the sinner).

31. See Exod 34:1–9; Num 14:12–20.

32. Lev 1:3–9. See generally Lev 1–5.

33. Ps 51:4,17–18. See also Jesus' admonition to the "woman caught in adultery" in John's gospel. ". . . Jesus was left alone with the woman standing before him. Jesus . . . said to her, 'Woman, where are they? Has no one condemned you?'. She said, 'No one, sir,'

As time wore on, Paul faced an even bigger problem than trying to reconcile the cross with Judaism's traditional beliefs: the delay of the second coming. No matter which of Paul's theories brought the potential convert to belief in Jesus as the Messiah, the underlying promise had always been that the reward for believing was to be assured of joining Christ in heaven on the last day. But, when Jesus failed to reappear, Paul had nothing to promise new converts as a reward for their believing any of his theories of the cross. Paul's solution to this problem was that the believer could be "raised in Christ" in the *here and now*.

> So if you have been raised in Christ, seek the things that are above, where Christ is, seated at the right hand of God. Set your minds on things that are above, not on things that are on earth, for you have died, and your life is hidden with Christ in God. When Christ who is your life is revealed, then you also will be revealed with him in glory.[34]

Salvation would no longer mean eternal life in heaven but a process of sanctification in which the new convert would "die" to the former pagan beliefs and culture and "live" as Jesus had lived, clothed "with compassion, kindness, humility, meekness, and patience . . ."[35] Indeed, throughout his later letters, Paul exhorted the new converts to live "in" Christ, to put on "the mind" of Christ, and to "live for the praise of his glory"[36] by actively seeking "spiritual wisdom and understanding."[37] They would thus, through God's grace, experience a "resurrection" in this life, living as "children of God," as spiritually transformed as the resurrected Jesus:

> From now on, therefore, we regard no one from a human point of view; even though we once knew Christ from a human point of view, we know him no longer in that way. So if anyone is in Christ, there is a new creation: everything old has passed away; see, everything has become new![38]

And Jesus said, 'Neither do I condemn you. Go your way, and from now on do not sin again'" (John 8:10-12).

34. Col 3:1-4.
35. Col 3:14.
36. Eph 1:12.
37. Col 1:3-4, 9-10.
38. 2 Cor 5:16-17.

Thus, while both Paul and Jesus believed that God was more concerned with establishing loving, forgiving relationships than with judgment and retribution, and both believed in the centrality of conversion of the human heart in God's plan of redemption, Paul set Jesus' teachings off on a course Jesus would not have anticipated. From Jesus' teaching about the imminence of the apocalypse, the coming of the Son of Man, and the fulfillment of God's promises to Israel, Paul theorized that the apocalypse would arrive with the second coming of the warrior Messiah and would serve as the means by which righteous believers would attain eternal life. From Jesus' revelation of himself as a son of man, a prophet, and a rabbi, Paul found the Davidic Messiah and God's own Son. From Jesus' teachings about the kingdom of God, Paul envisioned a future where the kingdom of God was equivalent to "heaven" or full communion with the living Christ. And, from Jesus' willingness to accept his awful fate so as not to break the loving solidarity with God and with those who had believed in him, Paul created some complex atonement theories by which the cross had redeemed not only righteous Jews but all of humanity.

The New Theology in Context

We have now come a long way from the historical Jesus, an itinerant rabbi who was believed by his followers to be a future king. Paul's various extrapolations of Jesus' teachings, created in order to explain the resurrection and post-resurrection events, required the incorporation into Judaism of beliefs that were, for the most part, alien, if not repugnant, to his fellow Jews. That much can be deduced from Paul's mistreatment at the hands of his Jewish brethren (and Romans) chronicled in Acts. Moreover, as we will see, at least two of Paul's extrapolations would have been personally offensive to Jesus.

Reactions of Paul's Pagan Contemporaries

Paul's new audience comprised the inheritors of more than five hundred years of Greek systematic thought by such luminaries as Socrates, Plato, and Aristotle. For these Hellenists, a new system of thought about ancient questions would have been at least entertained in the spirit of intellectual curiosity. As for Paul's teaching that Jesus was a divine emissary of God, Greek and Roman culture had always believed in a permeable boundary between the divine and humankind. Gods routinely visited (and even cohabitated) with humans, and humans could share fully in their divinity and even ascend to their realms. Additionally, Paul's ransom and suffering servant theories of the cross would have seemed entirely consistent with the purpose of making sacrifices in pagan culture. For Greeks and Romans, the gods were above all unpredictable—occasionally vengeful and occasionally beneficent—so it was essential to the order and prosperity of their whole societies that a system of regular sacrifices be in place to pacify the gods' worst tendencies. Thus, for a pagan audience, Paul's Christology and his second two theories of salvation would have been both logical and familiar.

Reactions of Paul's Jewish Contemporaries

Of all the features of Paul's new theology that would have been most alien to his Jewish audiences, it would have been his claim that Jesus was the Messiah foretold by the prophets of old. In effect, Paul was asking his audiences to disregard centuries of learned scriptural interpretation and to reread the Hebrew scripture in a wholly novel way in light of the resurrection. And this rereading would not be about insignificant matters: It would concern the very cornerstone of hope that had sustained Israel over generations of subjugation and captivity.

In addition, Paul's "high Christology," which borders on claiming that Jesus—either during his lifetime or thereafter—embodied God's divine nature, would have been blasphemy to his fellow Jews. Paul's "low Christology" might have been perplexing but not inconceivable, given that Jewish tradition had always recognized that God's spirit can reach deeply into the heart and that the righteous would be raised in bodily form at the end time.

Paul's Jewish audience might also have welcomed Paul's teaching about the possibility of mystical sanctification during one's earthly life. Yahweh's transformative power is clearly attested to in Hebrew scripture—including the transformation of Moses from his former life as an Egyptian adoptee, a murderer, and an incompetent spokesperson to the holiest leader/visionary in Israel's history. Moreover, although Judaism did not establish a distinct mystical tradition until the Middle Ages (*Kabbalah*), the understanding was that a mystical tradition had long existed within the sacred scriptures and had been recognized at various times in different forms, one of which was during the Second Temple period when Jesus was alive.[39]

39. Second-temple Judaism produced a number of mystical (and wisdom) texts, most notably the book of Daniel (which Jesus was said to have quoted when asked by

CHAPTER 9 PAUL'S WITNESS

Jesus' Reaction

It is, of course, impossible to know what the historical Jesus would have made of Paul's theology. Their differing teaching styles clearly reveal their differing senses of purpose, making any comparative approach both speculative and unfair. Jesus was a teacher who tried to reach the human heart by telling stories grounded in his listeners' everyday lives. Paul was an evangelist who created brilliant arguments to support his belief that Jesus was the Jewish Messiah and had solved the problem of sin. While Jesus used catchy phrases to help his listeners remember his wisdom, Paul used the tools of Pharisaic logic and textual exegesis to win over his listeners' minds. For Jesus, God was to be *experienced* as much through the majesty of God's creation—such as the flowers in the fields—as through the justice and mercy inherent in God's laws.[40] For Paul, however, God was not so much a verb to be experienced in everyday life as a noun to be probed and defined.

Yet, if we take Jesus seriously as a teacher of a reformed kind of Judaism, we can make some educated guesses about aspects of Paul's theology that would, for Jesus, have been beyond the pale. For example, it is inconceivable that the historical Jesus would have believed that he was equal to God, whether in nature or in attribute, much less that he was a timeless Being who had co-existed with God for all eternity. We have already noted that many Jewish holy people were called "sons" of God—including prophets, kings, and sages—and that the anticipated Jewish Messiah was never equated with God. Even most fundamentally, Judaism's central claim that distinguishes it from the surrounding pagan cultures is that God is one, indivisible, and wholly other than humankind. It is thus impossible for God to have a human son as kin—whether spiritually or physically. Human beings might share some of the qualities attributed to God, or they might be empowered by God's Spirit to act for God, but it would have been apostasy to believe that a human being could completely share God's divine nature.[41]

Pilate who he was) and the book of Enoch, with its elaborate descriptions of demonology and the coming Messianic age. The stories told about Jesus' own transformation from village artisan to the embodiment of sacrificial love fit nicely within this tradition of Jewish mysticism.

40. For more insight into the emerging field of cosmogenesis, see Rahner, *Foundations of Christian Faith*, and Swimme, *The Universe Is a Green Dragon*.

41. In fact, one of the primary reasons early Christians were persecuted was their refusal to worship Caesar Augustus, who had declared himself to be a god.

Moreover, we have already noted that there is scant evidence that Jesus believed that he was the Son of Man in the cosmic sense and no evidence that Jesus would have believed that the Messiah was the same figure as the Son of Man. In Jesus' estimation, the Messiah was a godly warrior for Israel's freedom, while the Son of Man was the herald of the end times. Additionally, even if Jesus believed that he was the long-awaited Messiah, he could not have believed either in the Messiah's resurrection or his second coming, for two reasons. First, there was no belief in Judaism that the Messiah would come a second time nor that the Messiah would be resurrected. Second, if Paul was correct and Jesus, as Messiah, would either act like or actually be the cosmic, war-like Son of Man, it would directly contradict Jesus' teachings about the power of salvific love and nonviolent social change. Parenthetically, this would also directly contradict the theology of the earliest church that Jesus was a gentle, persecuted "suffering servant" type of Messiah!

Moreover, Jesus would have been stricken by Paul's omission of his teachings about the kingdom of God—the vision that animated Jesus' entire life. On the other hand, Jesus did embrace the idea of transformation through a process of sanctification, even though he would have rejected the idea that the Kingdom was a future spiritual reality. For Jesus, the Kingdom would be a community affair in which God's desire for justice, prosperity, and peace would finally be realized. The path of transformation Jesus outlined in his Sermon on the Mount would be the "way" the Kingdom would finally come and not an end in itself.[42]

Underlying Assumptions

As previously noted, the disciples could have simply dispersed after Jesus' death. But they continued to meet and to pray, constructing an image of the Messiah that tied them to the Jewish prophecies. In fact, from the beginning of Jesus' ministry, no one questioned that Jewish prophecy was the *only* mirror through which to interpret Jesus' identity and the significance of his teaching. This is not surprising, of course, but it begs the question of whether, after the resurrection and post-resurrection events, Christianity

---

42. It is unclear why Paul did not preach the same "good news" to the new converts that Jesus had taught and witnessed; whether this was because Paul never heard about it from the disciples, did not understand it, or believed that it had become irrelevant in light of the resurrection cannot be known.

CHAPTER 9 PAUL'S WITNESS

might have gone in another direction—one more faithful to what Jesus actually taught and that we see captured in the Gospel of John.

The determination to anchor the Jesus narrative within Judaism—instead of seeing Judaism as informing a new revelation of God—had four momentous consequences for the evolving shape of the new faith. The first consequence is that Paul had to somehow reconcile the ancient texts about the messianic promise to the events he had experienced. In other words, Paul had to create "theology"—the art of scriptural interpretation as it relates to unfolding history—so that a new, composite vision of God's messianic purposes could be formulated. Thus, whereas Judaism was and is a faith tradition built on God's promises and Israel's lived response to these promises, Christianity became a religion based upon believing a certain theology. As the second consequence, which is related to the first one, by looking backward instead of forward for a context within which to understand the miraculous events of the resurrection and post-resurrection appearances, the disciples limited the revelation of God in history to Jewish history, thereby foreclosing the option of a new revelation going forward within the context of their own time. To seal the deal, the early church fathers closed the New Testament canon in the late 300s at the councils of Hippo and Carthage.[43]

The third momentous consequence for emerging Christianity was that the disciples, in order to form a theology, had to approach their own scripture differently. Rather than reading it as a chronicle of call and response or as the basis for hope in the fulfillment of God's promises, the disciples searched backwards into scripture to locate proof texts for their spiritual experiences. To be clear, the practice of looking back into Hebrew scripture in order to discover how it might apply to present circumstances is what Jewish sages have always done. But, by the time Luke wrote Acts, the prevailing belief was not only that Hebrew scripture informed the new sect but that it actually *predicted and found its fulfillment* in the coming of Jesus, the Messiah. Two stories in Acts make this point clearly. The first is a story of Jesus' dejected followers on the road to Emmaus where a mysterious stranger "opened up" the Hebrew scripture, showing the travelers how Hebrew scripture had predicted the crucifixion.[44] In the second story, the apostle Philip encounters a eunuch from Ethiopia beside the road. The eunuch is confused about the meaning of the "suffering servant" passages

---

43. The Jewish canon was closed with the writing of Ezra/Nehemiah in c. 300 BCE.
44. Luke 24:13.

in Isaiah, and Philip interprets it to foretell the events of Jesus' and resurrection—at which point, the eunuch is baptized into the new sect.[45]

James Carroll and others[46] have attributed this practice to competition between Jewish Pharisees and the new Jewish Jesus sect after the destruction of the Jerusalem temple in 70 CE, roughly contemporaneously with Mark's Gospel. The destruction of the temple by the Romans, never to be rebuilt, forced the relocation of cultic worship to local synagogues—which is where Jesus' apostles were also teaching. In the skirmish for converts, the Jesus sect had to convince their fellow Jews that Yahweh had done something new in Jesus; that the only way to salvation came through belief in him as the Messiah; and that Hebrew scripture had always predicted the very life, death, and resurrection they had personally witnessed. In addition, if Jesus was the Davidic Messiah, that must mean that it would be Jesus who, on the apocryphal Day of the Lord, would rescue all righteous believers from the throes of death—Jesus having been the "first fruits" of those who would eventually be raised to live with him in "eternal life."

Supersessionism reached its pinnacle when the gospels proclaimed that Jesus was not only the Messiah but the son of God (though this was to be secret knowledge, according to Mark's Gospel). By circa 100 CE, when John's gospel was written, not only was this Jesus the Messiah but he was also the *only* son of God, co-equal with God and existing as God's "Word" for all time until he was incarnated as Jesus of Nazareth. Thus, Jesus, as the Word of God, had always been present in Hebrew scripture. Even as early as circa 80 CE, the writer of the first epistle to Peter wrote, "Concerning . . . salvation, the prophets who prophesied of the grace that was to be yours made careful search and inquiry, inquiring about the person or time that the *Spirit of Christ within them* indicated when it testified in advance to the sufferings destined for Christ and the subsequent glory . . ."[47] (emphasis added).

Not only, then, did the Hebrew prophets have Jesus in mind when they prophesied about the coming Messiah, but they, too, were filled with the "spirit of Christ" (whether they knew it or not), and it was that spirit and not the collective wisdom of Jewish thinkers and chroniclers that made the prophecy reliable. By the time Bishop Ignatius of Antioch was on his way to execution in Rome, believers were being cautioned, "Never

---

45. Acts 8:35.
46. Carroll, *Constantine's Sword*. See also Boys, *Has God Only One Blessing?*
47. 1 Pet 1:8–11.

allow yourselves to be led astray by false teachings and antiquated and useless fables. Nothing of any use can be got from them. If we are still living in the practice of Judaism, it is an admission that we have failed to receive the gift of grace."[48]

Related to this impact is that converts to the new covenant came to rely on different written sources than the Hebrew scripture for spiritual guidance and inspiration, beginning with Paul's letters and the various hymns that were circulating among the early house churches. Over time, Hebrew scripture took second place as the "old covenant" to the "new covenant" of Christian writings. Hebrew scripture was no longer viewed as the dispositive source of spiritual wisdom but was seen as useful only to confirm, justify, and validate the new Christian gospel. This would eventually lead to the Christian belief that its own new scripture supersedes and is more enlightened than God's revelation to Israel. An extreme outcome of this belief was the teaching of a very early Christian theologian Marcion of Sinope (85–160 CE). Marcion considered himself a follower of Paul, whom he believed was the only true apostle of Jesus Christ because he worshiped the only true God—the loving God of the new covenant, and not the vengeful God of the old. Marcion compiled perhaps the first canon of Christian sacred scripture, which included only the Pauline epistles and the Gospel of Marcion, an edited version of Luke's Gospel.

In the fourth and final consequence, Paul fundamentally changed the focus and purpose of leading a religious life. For Jesus, the purpose of religious observance was primarily to guide the believer in walking the "way" of love and humble surrender, thus creating a feedback loop for the transformation of Israel as a whole. As the hearts of individuals changed and as Israel's heart softened, the transformation of Israel would be actualized in the here and now. For Paul, on the other hand, it was all about personal salvation and the personality cult of Jesus Christ. The purpose of leading a sinless life was to prepare for an afterlife with Christ at his second coming. Gone was Jesus' joy in the moment—in eating and drinking, in awakening to the majesty of God's creation, and in participating in and being formed by a close community of friends. In its place, a religious culture suspicious of human sensuality, obsessed with right belief, and focused on suffering and death took hold. We have been living these consequences ever since.

Seeing the Jesus narrative as the outcome of ancient prophecies was but one of the assumptions underlying Paul's theology. Two other powerful

---

48. Ignatius of Antioch, *Epistle to the Magnesians.*

influencers also played their role: Paul's preference for "high" over "low" Christology and his determination to carry forward the imperative of the justice of God over God's love. Regarding Christology, Paul came perilously close to claiming that both the crucified and the risen Jesus were divine. Jesus was not, according to Paul, a mere "son" of God, as David had been and as the Davidic Messiah would be. God had offered up his "Christ" for crucifixion and it was that "Christ" that rose from the dead. This Christ was Messiah, the "Son of God," and a "life-giving spirit" whose origin was in heaven. Scholars have characterized this understanding of Jesus' personage as "high Christology," meaning that God had poured his divine nature into the human Jesus, so that he was divine from the moment of conception, while also sharing in the complete human experience. This understanding of Jesus' persona is contrasted with "low Christology," which sees Jesus as a fully fledged historical human being, albeit uniquely gifted with divine insight and power, who was transformed in his resurrection into "Christ."

In addition, the idea that God's justice requires payment for human transgression in order to restore the broken relationship with God (i.e., restore "at-one-ment" with God) clearly would have resonated deeply with Paul's Jewish audience because of the centrality of the temple sacrificial rites to Jewish Second Temple observance. Yet, Jesus' teaching proclaims the imperative of love over justice and, as noted earlier, Jesus did not go to the cross thinking that God's justice was somehow being done through his death. Far from it! Moreover, Paul's teaching that this particular and unique sacrifice was God's way of bringing *the entire sacrificial system both to its climax and to its close* would have been unthinkable. Finally, according to Paul, this "Son" was not only the definitive sacrificial "Lamb of God" but also sufficient atonement *for the aggregate sin of all humanity.*[49]

---

49. Paul's new theology of atonement resonates with us today, particularly in evangelical circles. It provides a biblically based answer to the age-old problem of sin, and it logically explains the unjust death of God's anointed. Yet, it contradicts the gospels' portrayal of Jesus' teaching about the possibility of human transformation in the present and Paul's conviction that Jesus' death was necessary in order for the Spirit to be activated and for the Christ to be revealed.

Chapter 10   Toward a New Orthodoxy

THIS JOURNEY HAS CONVINCED me that we need a new way of interpreting the Jesus narrative, one that opens up the possibility of ongoing divine revelation. As it happens, there is an alternative way to present the Jesus narrative—both in terms of interpretive approach and analytical assumptions. Most of us are familiar with the expression "paradigm shift," but perhaps fewer of us understand where that came from and why it opens up a new way of comprehending the Jesus narrative. This journey has also convinced me that much of what Paul taught would have been alien—even blasphemous—to Jesus.

In this last chapter, we will explore the possibility that the Kuhnian approach to understanding the Jesus narrative might offer us a way to see it as both revolutionary and ongoing. We will also look at how Paul's theology was received by his fellow Jews and speculate about what Jesus might have thought of it. Last, we'll consider how we might reinvent Christianity so that it more closely reflects what Jesus taught and died for.

Paradigm Change

The phrase "paradigm change" comes from the work of Thomas Kuhn, a physicist turned science historian, whose work, *The Structure of Scientific Revolutions*,[1] changed the way we understand how science moves forward. Before Kuhn, the overwhelming consensus about the scientific method was championed by Karl Popper, a professor of logic and science

---

1. Kuhn, *Structure of Scientific Revolutions*, 54.

at the London School of Economics. Many of us learned it in grade school: Science begins with problems and then proceeds via conjecture and refutation.[2] The best science occurs when scientists propose bold theories and test them but give them up if they are falsified. For Popper, scientific inquiry is always contextual—that is, what might be true in one context might not be true in another—and scientific "truth" is that which has been resistant to falsification over time.

Kuhn built his theory of the evolution of scientific knowledge on Popper's work. Kuhn posits that what we take to be "normal science" is actually the socialization of scientists by accepted paradigms. Paradigms are common intellectual frameworks, "universally recognized scientific achievements that, for a time, provide model problems and solutions for a community of practitioners . . . ."[3] Progress in scientific thought occurs through puzzle solving, in which new information is tested against the prevailing paradigm and, if found to be anomalous, is resolved either by incorporating it into the existing paradigm or by discovering experimental error. But, over long periods of time, discrepancies in the existing paradigm that cannot be resolved accumulate and eventually reach a point at which some scientists begin to question the paradigm itself. At this point, the discipline enters a period of crisis, following which a new world view, or paradigm, emerges—one that subsumes the old results with the anomalous results to become a new paradigm. This, Kuhn calls "revolutionary science."

In the years since Kuhn and Popper wrote about the evolution of scientific thought, Kuhn's approach has caught hold as particularly enlightening within the context of the social sciences. As we consider the extent to which Kuhn's insights might apply to understanding God's plan in and through the life of Jesus, it will be recalled that Judaism shares more of the features of a social science than those of a religion, in that it encompasses a complete lifestyle, including its own unique socio-economic, moral, and legal systems.

The Kuhnian approach to understanding historical/social evolution is more than just a handy way to see how Jewish thought might have evolved; it is wholly consistent with Judaism's own understanding of how God acts in history and how history itself unfolds. Judaism understands history as mysteriously ordered by God, while always evolving through crisis to redemption, toward a new revelation of who God is and what God's purposes

---

2. Popper, *Conjectures and Refutations*, 35.
3. Kuhn, *Structure of Scientific Revolutions*, vii.

are for his chosen people. History would reach "fulfillment" in the messianic age—that eternal vanishing point when Yahweh's hopes and promises to Israel would be a living reality. Within this framework, the progression of time was understood as cyclical, marked by the seven annual ritual observances around agriculture. Three of these—Passover (*Pesach*), Weeks (Pentecost or *Shavuot*), and Booths (*Sukkoth*)—were pilgrimage festivals, requiring the faithful to journey to the temple.[4] In addition, within the three major festivals were the biennial celebrations of the harvests of barley and wheat and the annual ingathering of grapes, olives, and other fruits of the land.[5,6] Clearly, Jesus and his contemporaries would not have understood history as linear in any sense.

Applying Kuhn's approach, we might see first-century Judaism, with all of its expectations associated with the coming of the Davidic Messiah-king, as the normative paradigm for many centuries. We might also see all of the set-backs the Jewish people faced over those centuries—multiple invasions, natural disasters, and reversions to pagan practices—as anomalies to the unfolding of the messianic paradigm, with it being the role of the prophets to integrate those anomalies into that paradigm. But we might also see that there came a point when a discrepancy in the paradigm was so disruptive that it placed the paradigm in crisis. For Jesus' followers, that point was Jesus' shameful death and resurrection. After those events, it was no longer possible to hold that anomaly within the paradigm of the Davidic Messiah-king who was supposed to triumph over Israel's oppressors and whose resurrection was not part of Jewish prophecy. Eventually, a new paradigm—Jesus as a universal, suffering, servant messiah whose promise was personal salvation—gained acceptance, subsuming the former paradigm and challenging it to change. To be clear, this did not mean that Jesus' followers believed that the post-Easter events superseded the ancient prophecies concerning a Davidic Messiah-king or rejected the Davidic Messiah-king as Yahweh's true promise to Israel. Rather, the events they had witnessed convinced them that Yahweh had acted in new and startling ways within the old paradigm.

---

4. Passover also commemorates the exodus from Egypt, while Weeks celebrates the giving of Torah to Moses, and Booths recalls the dwelling of the Israelites in booths during their sojourn in the wilderness.

5. Exod 23:14–23; Lev 23:5 *et seq.*

6. Lev 23:42.

To restate this point, this new messianic revelation, arising from the resurrection and post-resurrection events, is not a rejection of Judaism and its rich source of wisdom and spiritual inspiration. Nor is it a grafting onto the messianic expectations of Israel gaining a new type of messiah—a suffering, resurrected servant. Rather, it is the emergence of an entirely new messianic model, one that was not prophesied but, like Jesus himself, is firmly rooted in the God of Israel and the teachings of Judaism. Indeed, Jesus himself seems to have understood this critical point. When asked why his disciples did not observe traditional rules of fasting, Jesus replied,

> No one sews a piece of unshrunk cloth on an old cloak, for the patch pulls away from the cloak, and a worse tear is made. Neither is new wine put into old wineskins, otherwise the skins burst, and the wine is spilled, and the skins are destroyed; but new wine is put into fresh wineskins and *both are preserved* [italics added].[7]

Jesus seems to have understood himself and his message to be the new wine—new kind of messiah—that would be necessary in order to receive and teach God's latest revelation—the good news.

To conclude and in summary, we can see that the attempts made by the apostles and gospel writers to characterize the resurrection and ensuing events as both predicted by Hebrew scripture and historically factual are wholly unpersuasive. Nevertheless, we can approach these events confident of their truth because they clearly have historical value with respect to both Judaism and the evolution of Christianity. Moreover, although the historical/critical approach cannot, by definition, account for non-factual, purely spiritual experience, we now have the Kuhnian "revolutionary" approach to guide our inquiry into the post-resurrection events. This approach understands history as both evolutionary and driven by a God who is both dynamic and adaptive.

Within the larger framework of Christianity's evolution from Judaism, the Kuhnian model also explains how, after Jesus' death and resurrection, his followers were able to integrate those events into the normative Jewish paradigm of a Davidic Messiah-king so that they still considered themselves Jews. But, as more and more joined the Jewish Jesus movement, and as the risen Jesus was seen more and more as a deity—the Son of God—and not only a risen messiah, the disruption to Judaism's fundamental strict

---

7. Matt 9:16.

CHAPTER 10   TOWARD A NEW ORTHODOXY

monotheism was too great to incorporate the new anomaly, and the split between Christianity and Judaism became inevitable.

Seeds of a New Orthodoxy

Trying to free Jesus' teachings from the overlay of Paul's theology is difficult because it touches on Christianity's core orthodoxy—who Jesus was, what he believed his mission to be, and the significance of the cross and resurrection. Moreover, Paul's theology served to foreshadow some of the earliest doctrines in Christianity, among them that heaven is a locale to aspire to, the deification (not just divinization) of Jesus, the idea of a trinitarian God, and the conviction that Christianity supersedes Judaism as God's latest revelation to humankind. At the same time, Paul's failure to ground his theology in transformative experience as opposed to right belief meant that Jesus' teaching about God's desire for human wholeness and the possibility of the realization of the kingdom of God in the here and now was utterly lost. From its earliest days, Christianity became a religion about belief in Jesus as Savior rather than the experience of God "among" us.[8]

Equally tragically, by casting out the "law" as the instrument of holiness and salvation, Paul diminished the value of praxis in the path of transformation. The laws of Judaism were designed to prescribe practices that would ensure the sanctification of daily living, but Paul taught sanctification through right belief and the grace of God.[9] Christianity thus became more about believing than about leading a disciplined life of contemplation and action.

More broadly, had the disciples and gospel writers had the benefit of seeing God's revelation in Jesus as revolutionary in the Kuhnian sense, Christianity as it has been practiced for a millennium would look more like the disruptive good news of a Jewish rabbi than a faith tradition preoccupied with remodeling the Davidic Messiah-king so as to explain Jesus' death and resurrection. The Kuhnian approach would have offered them—and now offers us—a way to honor the reality of a genuine spiritual experience that is by definition not fact-based. It sees "truth" as a cultural/social construct and what is held to be "true" as evolutionary. Not insignificantly, it directly

---

8. Luke 21.

9. It took the church another 1100 years to come up with a doctrine that brought praxis and belief together in a single theory of grace working on praxis to the end of the transformation of human consciousness. See Aquinas, *Theological Texts*.

confronts supersessionism by recognizing that no paradigm is "wrong" so long as it is rationally based on what was known at a particular time.

Moreover, the determination to interpret the Jesus narrative through the lens of Jewish prophetic expectations had additional consequences for the future character of Christianity. We have already noted that the anomaly of Jesus' death within the Davidic construct of the Messiah required some explanation. But this had the unfortunate effect of focusing everyone's attention on Jesus' suffering and death—its purpose and meaning—rather than Jesus' life. It served to distort the salvific message of the good news as Jesus preached and lived it into theories about death, suffering, and the cross. One need only look at the composition of all of the gospels to note that the events of Jesus' last days occupy nearly one-third of the entire text.

Throughout, I have been troubled by a final question. Does any of this matter? The answer is that it matters because the central claim of Christianity—that Jesus Christ was the Davidic Messiah—is clearly false. Christianity has tried to have it both ways: a faith tradition that claims Jewish biblical roots while simultaneously denying the wisdom of those roots as they pertain to the Messiah. Thus, for example, we have Paul's teaching that Jesus was the cosmic Son of Man who would return to usher in a new age and the church's belief in the second coming, while, at the same time, we have scant evidence that Jesus was the cosmic Son of Man, and we know that the Jewish sacred texts clearly differentiate between prophecies about the Messiah and those about the Son of Man. We also have Paul's sidelining of Jesus' teaching about the kingdom of God and the Church's resulting adoption of a theology of personal salvation through faith and grace, instead of Jesus' vision of communal salvation through personal conversion.

Does this mean that Paul was just flat out misguided and that his entire theology should be jettisoned? No, for three reasons. First, despite these losses, there was also a monumental gain. Paul made explicit what the gospel writers (except John) either chose to ignore or did not understand: that Jesus was a mystic and that his "way" was the path to spiritual transformation. "Above all," Paul writes in his letter to the Colossians, "clothe yourselves with love, which binds everything together in perfect harmony. And let the peace of Christ rule in your hearts, to which indeed you were called in the one body. And be thankful."[10] Second, Paul is not responsible

---

10. Col 3:14–15. This is one of Paul's later letters and was probably not written by him. It serves, however, as one of the primary source materials for the claim made by Richard Rohr and Matthew Fox that Christ is a cosmic phenomenon. See Rohr's *The Universal Christ* and Fox's *Coming of the Cosmic Christ*: "The Cosmic Christ ushers in

CHAPTER 10 TOWARD A NEW ORTHODOXY

for what became of his theology in the hands of the early church fathers. For example, Paul did not actually teach that God has a trinitarian nature, even though he did refer to Jesus Christ as God's "Son" and to God's "Spirit" as a distinct entity. The issue of the nature of God actually remained unresolved for over three hundred years, during which time competing forms of Christianity held sway in much of the Roman Empire.[11] And third, Paul was right about the big picture: God's plan for humankind is the good news, as witnessed by Jesus himself, both as he lived and after he died.

Thus, the real good news is full of hope for humankind. It is grounded in human experience, the potential for evolution of consciousness, and practical wisdom. It is accessible to all, not just some. It is the ultimate answer to humankind's longing for wholeness and intimacy with God. It is faithful to Judaism in its assumptions about the nature of God and God's desire for His creation, but it is honest about the reality that God was revealing an entirely new plan for humankind in the life and witness of Jesus Christ. The bad news is that I have never heard this good news preached.

Now that we have a new tool to interpret how truth can evolve over time and can encompass truth that is both spiritual and historically factual, we can at last draw a picture of what Christian orthodoxy might have been, had there been no assumption that Jesus' identity and mission

---

an era of coherence . . . The Cosmic Christ unites psyche and cosmos once again . . . The opposite of cohesion is chaos . . . One way the Cosmic Christ moves us from chaos to cohesion is by bringing hope—hope that coherence is possible—back to the psyche and thus back to the human race and its institutions" (Fox, *Coming of the Cosmic Christ*, 135). The theologian Teilhard de Chardin wrote that Christ has a cosmic body as well as a mystical body. See Teilhard de Chardin, "La Vie Cosmique," 67–69.

11. Four theories about the relationship between God and Christ predominated. Docetism taught that Jesus had not been a human being but was, rather, God merely in the form of a human being. Separatism taught that Jesus was both human and divine, so that when the human Jesus died, the divine Jesus continued to live. Modalism, one of the most popular theologies, held that God was One but could manifest Godself in different ways, just as water (H_2O) can manifest itself as liquid, steam, or ice, though each form remains H_2O. The fourth theology was Arianism. This was the most widespread belief, and it endured long after the Council of Nicaea, held in 325, declared it a heresy. Arianism held that Jesus was a fully divine personage and had co-existed with God for an eternity. But Jesus was also "begotten" by God—God had created him at some point in time—and, as such, Jesus Christ was neither consubstantial nor co-eternal with God but was a lesser form of the divine. The compromise reached at Nicaea is similar to that proclaimed in the gospel of John (although absent in the synoptic gospels)—namely, that Jesus was God's very "Word" and, though begotten of God, had co-existed with God for all eternity: "God from God, Light from Light, True God from True God" ("Nicene Creed," in *The Book of Common Prayer*, 358).

were delimited by Jewish prophecy and had Paul trusted the reality of his own spiritual experience instead of writing a complicated theology of high Christology that Jesus himself would not have believed. If we imagine that God, in resurrecting Jesus, intended that we should see the fullness of who Jesus really was, we can also see that the revelation of God in Jesus Christ unfolded in two segments—the life and death of Jesus, a living mystic, and his resurrection as the mystical Christ. The one doesn't exclude the other; that is, the historical and the mystical Jesus were always the same historical personage while Jesus was alive, but it took his resurrection in order for the full revelation of his mystical self to emerge. There never was an historical Jesus who was not in loving union with God, whether as a human being or as a resurrected being. Jesus' mission, whether during his mortal life or now, during his eternal life, was always to respond to the yearning of our hearts for the same mystical union with God by showing us how to practice love.

It is only when Jesus' identity and mission are understood in this way that we can reconstruct what a revitalized Christianity might look like. It would look decidedly Jewish, with Judaism's beliefs in the inherent goodness of all of God's creation, the truth that God's creativity is accessible and interwoven with the events of our lives, the reality that God's spirit can inhabit human consciousness and change us into "sons" of God, and the possibility of human transformation through a process of healing and reconciliation. But it would also be startling good news that God is now seeking us as individuals, with a promise of mystical union with and in Christ, and with a mission to bind us together as a universal community committed to social justice and peace. In short, Christianity would look a lot like the millennial wedding that began this journey.

Afterword

THE FADED FRESCOES ON the wall of the Christian catacombs in Rome, the burial locale of the second generation of Christians, show us various images of salvation, such as Jonah's deliverance from the belly of the whale and Daniel's deliverance from the lion's den. This is extraordinarily significant for two reasons. First, the earliest Christians looked to the Hebrew scriptures—not to other writings—for their understanding of salvation. It was there that they found images of deliverance from evil—not complicated beliefs about the significance of the cross. Second, while this seems odd to us now, the earliest Christians did not celebrate the Incarnation (i.e., Christmas) as a day separate from the date of the Epiphany (i.e., the manifestation of the Christ light within Jesus of Nazareth).[1] In other words, the earliest Christians were not as concerned with the issue of Jesus' historical identity, his mission, and his death as we are today; rather, they were focused on what God had accomplished in Jesus' life and, above all, in his resurrection and post-resurrection appearances.

At the end of this seven-year journey, I have become convinced that, if we are to be truly faithful to who Jesus was and believed himself to be, we must unpack the religious/cultural assumptions that created the identity we have come to associate with him. We must take a fresh look at what Jesus actually taught, what he actually did as he roamed the Palestinian countryside, and what God perfected in him through his death and resurrection. If we do that, we might come out with a Christianity that truly is *good news*—not only for millennials but for generations to come.

1. Grabar, *Christian Iconography*, 12–13.

Bibliography

American-Israeli Cooperative Enterprise (AICE). "Anointing." *Jewish Virtual Library*. https://www.jewishvirtuallibrary.org/anointing.
American-Israeli Cooperative Enterprise (AICE). "Forgiveness." *Jewish Virtual Library*. https://www.jewishvirtuallibrary.org/forgiveness.
Anderson, Bernard W. *Understanding the Old Testament*. New Jersey: Prentice-Hall, 1986.
Anonymous. *The Cloud of Unknowing*, ed. Evelyn Underhill. London: J. M. Watkins, 1946.
Arendt, Hannah. *Eichmann in Jerusalem: A Report on the Banality of Evil*. London: Penguin Classics, 1963.
Aquinas, Thomas. *Theological Texts*, ed. Thomas Gilby. London: Routledge, 1963.
Ben Avraham of Gerona, Yonah. *The Gates of Repentance*, translated by Shraga Silverstein. Jerusalem: Feldheim, 1971.
Ben Avraham, Shelomo. "Qorbanot: Sacrifices and Offerings." In *Torah 101*, Berkeley: The Mamre Institute for Jewish Studies, 2012.
Blomberg, Craig. "Jesus, Sinners and Table Fellowship." *Bulletin for Biblical Research* 19 (2009) 35.
Borg, Marcus. *Meeting Jesus Again for the First Time: The Historical Jesus and the Heart of Contemporary Faith*. San Francisco: HarperCollins, 1995.
———. *Jesus*. San Francisco: Harper Collins, 2006.
Boys, Mary C. *Has God Only One Blessing? Judaism as a Source of Christian Understanding*. NY: Paulist, 2000.
Collins, Raymond F. *Introduction to the New Testament*. NY: Doubleday, 1987.
Carroll, James. *Constantine's Sword*. Boston: Houghton Mifflin, 2001.
Crossan, John Dominic, and Sarah Sexton Crossan. *Resurrecting Easter: How the West Lost and the East Kept the Original Easter*. NY: HarperOne, 2018.
De Chardin, Teilhard. "La Vie Cosmique." In *Ecrits du Temps de la Guerre*, Paris: Editions de Seuil, 1965.
Douglas, Mary. *Purity and Danger*. London: Routledge, 1966.
Ehrman, Bart D. *Forged: Writing in the Name of God: Why the Bible's Authors Are Not Who We Think They Are*. NY: HarperOne, 2011.
———. *How Jesus Became God*. NY: HarperOne, 2014.

BIBLIOGRAPHY

Fox, Matthew. *The Coming of the Cosmic Christ: The Healing of Mother Earth and the Birth of a Global Renaissance*. San Francisco: Harper & Row, 1988.
Grabar, Andre. *Christian Iconography*. Princeton: Princeton University Press, 1968.
Heschel, Abraham Joshua. *The Sabbath*. Canada: HarperCollinsCanada, 1951.
The Hymnal 1982. NY: Church Hymnal Corp., 1985.
Ignatius of Antioch. "Epistle to the Magnesians." In *Early Christian Writings*, edited by Andrew Louth et al. London: Penguin Classics, 1968.
Jerusalem Talmud:y. Bik. 836–840.
Josephus, Flavius. *Antiquities*. 19.12.
Keating, Thomas. *Invitation to Love*. NY: Continuum, 2002.
Kittel, Gerhard, and Gerhard Friedrich. *Theological Dictionary of the New Testament*. Collegeville: Eerdmans, 1964.
Kuhn, Thomas. *The Structure of Scientific Revolutions*. Chicago: University of Chicago Press, 1970.
Levine, Amy-Jill. "Daniel." In *The New Oxford Annotated Bible With Apocryphal and Deuterocanonical Books*, edited by Michael Coogan et al. Oxford: University Press, 2003.
———. "The Many Faces of the Good Samaritan Most Wrong." *Biblical Archaeology Review* Jan/Feb (2012).
Mack, Burton L. *The Lost Gospel: The Book of Q*. San Francisco: HarperCollins, 1993.
Magness, Jodi. *Stone and Dung, Oil and Spit: Jewish Daily Life in the Time of Jesus*. Grand Rapids: Eerdmans, 2011.
Maimonides. *Mishneh Torah*.
Mechon Mamre. "Psalm 16:10." https://mechon-mamre.org/p/pt/pt2616.htm.
Merton, Thomas. *New Seeds of Contemplation*. NY: New Directions, 1949/2007.
Miller, Paul D. "God as Father: Seeing the Same God in Both Testaments." Nashville: The Ethics and Religious Liberty Commission, 2018.
Moller, Violet. *The Map of Knowledge: A Thousand-Year History of How Classical Ideas Were Lost and Found*. NY: Anchor, 2020.
Muhammad, Sardar, et al. "The Concept of Mystical Union: Juxtaposing Islamic and Christian Versions." In *Webology 18*, https://www.webology.org.
Murphy, Frederick J. *Early Judaism*. Peabody: Hendrickson, 2002.
"Nicene Creed." In *The Book of Common Prayer*, 358. New York: Oxford University Press, 1979.
Pliny the Elder. *Natural History 5*, translated by H. Rackham. Cambridge: Harvard University Press, 1952.
Popper, K. R. *Conjectures and Refutations*. London: Routledge, 1963.
Rahner, Karl. *Foundations of Christian Faith: An Introduction to the Idea of Christianity*. NY: Crossroad, 2004.
Reiser, William S. J. *Jesus in Solidarity with His People*. Collegeville, MN: Liturgical, 2000.
Rohr, Richard. *The Universal Christ*. NY: Convergent, 2021.
Sanders, E. P. *Jesus and Judaism*. Philadelphia: Fortress, 1985.
Schweitzer, Albert. *The Quest for the Historical Jesus*, translated by John Bowden et al. Minneapolis: Fortress, 2001.
Silber, Daniel S. "The Jewish Dietary Laws and Their Foundations." Third Year Paper, Harvard University School of Scholarly Communications, 1994.
Swimme, Brian. *The Universe is a Green Dragon: A Cosmic Creation Story*. Santa Fe, NM: Beal, 1984.

BIBLIOGRAPHY

Strong, James. *Strong's Exhaustive Concordance of the Bible.* Nashville: Thomas Nelson, 2009.

Tickle, Phyllis. *The Great Emergence: How Christianity is Changing and Why.* Grand Rapids: Baker, 2012.

Walke, Bruce K. "Heart." https://www.biblestudytools.com/dictionary/heart.

Wenham, Gordon I. "The Theology of Unclean Food." *The Evangelical Quarterly* 53 (1981).

Wigoder, Geoffrey "Forgiveness." In *Encyclopedia Judaica.* NY: AICE, 2007.

Wright, N. T. *Paul for Everyone: 1 Corinthians.* Westminster: John Knox, 2001.

———. *Jesus and the Victory of God.* Minneapolis: Fortress, 1996.

www.ingramcontent.com/pod-product-compliance
Lightning Source LLC
Chambersburg PA
CBHW071212160426

43196CB00011B/2266